Find Lasting LOVE

DICK PURNELL

HARVEST HOUSE™ PUBLISHERS

EUGENE, OREGON

Cover by Left Coast Design, Portland, Oregon

Cover photo by Nicolas Russell, The Image Bank

FINDING A LASTING LOVE
Copyright © 2003 by Dick Purnell
Published by Harvest House Publishers
Eugene, Oregon 97402

Library of Congress Cataloging-in-Publication Data

Purnell, Dick.
    [Becoming a friend & lover]
    Finding a lasting love / Dick Purnell.
        p. cm.
Originally published: Becoming a friend & lover. Updated ed. Nashville : T. Nelson, © 1995.
    Includes bibliographical references.
    ISBN 0-7369-1080-8 (pbk.)
    1. Single people--Religious life. 2. Mate selection—Religious aspects—
Christianity. 3. Dating (Social customs)—Religious aspects—Christianity.
    I. Title.
    BV4596.S5 P87 2003
    158.2—dc21

                                                                    2002015724

Printed in the United States of America.

04 05 06 07 08 09 10 / DP-KB / 10 9 8 7 6 5 4 3

To Paula

I am grateful to God that I found you—
and that His love will bind us together for life.
It is wonderful to be married to my best friend.

Contents

1. The Search for a Love Worthy of Your Life 11
2. The Foundation for a Lasting Love 21

Part One: A Balanced Relationship Star
3. Components of Oneness 41
4. Your Social Life: Having Real Fun 65
5. Your Mental Life:
   Discovering How You Think. 87
6. Your Emotional Life:
   Understanding Your Feelings 99
7. Your Physical Life:
   Expressing Love Creatively. 117
8. Your Spiritual Life: Exploring Your Souls 139

Part Two: Hindrances to a Lasting Love
9. Shutting Off Transparency 163
10. Pressing for Instant Intimacy 177
11. Saying Yes and Being Sorry. 191
12. Expecting Only Time to Heal 215

Part Three: Becoming the Right Person
13. Build Qualities That Attract 231
14. Keep on the Right Path to the Right One 247
    Notes. 257

Foreword

■ ■ ■

Too bad Dick Purnell didn't write *Finding a Lasting Love* 20 years ago. He could have saved me from a lot of mistakes and a lot of pain! I would have seen that my "Relationship Star" was missing a few points! (You'll understand what I'm talking about when you hit chapter 3). In this book, Dick examines relationships from five key aspects: social, mental, emotional, physical, and spiritual. So often it is easy to concentrate on only one or two areas at the expense or exclusion of the others. In so doing, a relationship will be unbalanced and over time will become more and more unwieldy until it ultimately fails. I know. I tried it.

I admire Dick's transparency and vulnerability in this work. He shares from his heart several of his own dating experiences through his many years as a single adult. He has incredible insight into the woes and wonders of dating, having learned much from his experiences. Reading a book on dating and relationships written by a 20-something-year-old would make me think, *Just be patient*. But Dick had to be patient for 42 years (okay, so maybe he wasn't always patient!). That gave him a lot of time and many opportunities to live and learn about the mysteries of relationships. God ultimately blessed Dick with His very best for him— his wonderful wife, Paula. Their relationship developed slowly and cautiously. Their experience is encouraging and inspiring to me.

Dick has been my colleague and friend for several years. I know firsthand of his genuine passion for helping single adults make healthy and virtuous life choices. You'll see that for yourself in the pages that follow. And Dick doesn't gloss over difficult subjects—he is candid and frank about all areas of relationships. Take what you learn from this book to heart—apply it to all of your relationships. Allow God to craft you into the person He wants you to become. One day you will be grateful—and so will your future spouse.

Oh, and don't forget—be patient.

May God bless you.

Susan Goter
Managing Editor, Strategic Adult Ministries Journal

Acknowledgments

■ ■ ■

Writing a book takes a lot more than just an author. You would not be holding this book in your hands if it were not for lots of individuals helping me. Throughout the long process some special people worked diligently with passion and commitment. My deepest thanks and appreciation goes to...

- Christina Holder—this edition of the book bears testimony to your insightful suggestions and professional skills. Thank you also for the profound impact you have had in our daughters' lives. We feel as though you are a part of our family.

- Nick Harrison, Gene Skinner, Carolyn McCready, LaRae Weikert, and the Harvest House team—what a great group. You gave this book new life. Your energy, skills, and heart have launched a message that will help singles everywhere improve their relationships with the opposite sex and build strong marriages.

- Kris Swiatocho—you are far more than an excellent graphic designer. Your passion and drive to motivate singles to excellence and godliness is an inspiration to Paula and me. You have a big heart and vision. We are glad to be called your friends.

- Carol Douglass—your research was thorough, and your suggestions helped me to present some of the material with greater clarity and passion. You have been a friend to Paula for decades, and I am glad you are also my friend.

- Cindy Hoegg—the way you handle the details of our office releases me to build our ministry in lots of areas. Thanks for your diligence and tenacity in the little things.

- Barb Lane—the manuscript bears the imprint of your editing skills and passion for presenting truth in a relevant package.

- Tina Hood—thanks for typing my notes, arranging my speaking schedule, and handling hundreds of details to keep our ministry expanding.

- Marty Williams Anderson—you motivated me with your creative ideas, editorial comments, and faithfulness in producing the original book.

- Curt Anderson—thanks to you, all our ministry functions kept going smoothly while I studied and wrote.

- David Blackard—as we traveled together to my speaking engagements, you sacrificially and energetically assisted me and my family so that I could take time to research and write.

- Joe Carlin—I am grateful to you for proofreading the final manuscript and giving me several excellent suggestions to clarify key ideas. Our friendship means a lot to me.

- Paula Purnell—your encouragement motivated me to keep working, and your constructive critique of my ideas and writing helped me refine the message. Above all, our companionship and love have deepened as we worked together to produce this book to help others find a lasting love.

1

The Search for a Love Worthy of Your Life

■ ■ ■

When I wrote the first edition of this book (titled *Becoming a Friend and Lover*), I began by telling a story about Mark, a friend of mine who dated a lot but was becoming frustrated trying to find the right woman. In the 1980s, Mark fit perfectly into the dating scene—years ago, people actually went out on dates. These days, dating looks quite different, and for many singles, the dating scene is frustrating for a completely different reason.

Courtney is a single woman in her mid-20s who says the idea of two people going out on a real date has ceased to exist in the twenty-first century. Instead, the dating scene involves "going out, meeting someone, going home with them, and then...well, you know," she says.

Has dating really reached so low? Are the opportunities to form meaningful relationships really being replaced by meaningless physical encounters?

In a *USA Today* editorial, writer Laura Vanderkam pointed out that the custom of "hooking up," defined as any physical encounter without expectations afterward, "pervades college culture" and that dates are "passé." She bases her opinion on a study by author David Brooks about the dating scene among college kids today at Princeton University. According to him, this generation is full of what he calls "organization kids"—people whose parents have so flooded their lives with scheduling, pressure to succeed, and extracurricular activities that "they no longer have hours to spend wooing a lover." Instead, they hook up, and as Vanderkam points out, "hookups do satisfy biology, but the emotional detachment doesn't satisfy the soul."

Something seems to have gone very wrong somewhere along the line. Mark would probably be shocked. According to Courtney, despite her desire to date someone, few people are actually dating. "It's very exciting when one of my friends meets someone and has a date! It's a privilege!" she says. Single people today still desire to be valued and cared for by someone special and, ultimately, to have a committed, lasting relationship.

"Commitment is important to me, and I think to probably everyone because everyone wants someone to be committed and faithful to them. We all want to be loved," Courtney says.

If you're like Courtney—an adult, not married, and possibly not even dating someone seriously—it's hard to feel fulfilled. I know. I was single until the age of 42. Married people constantly told me that I needed to get married and settle down in order to find fulfillment in my life. Yet when I looked at the married people around me and their problems, I knew that marriage didn't automatically bring lasting satisfaction. It took something more than a wedding to do that.

So for years, I tried to ignore all the good-hearted encouragement to marry. During that time, I dated several women, but I was so involved in my work that I didn't feel an overwhelming desire to marry any of them and face the potential of trading one set of problems for another. Although my work gave me great satisfaction and I saw no immediate reason for marrying, I did sense a desire to open my life to someone. I wanted to find out what another person was like and to have that person to know what I was like. But did I dare open myself to another person and risk my future happiness?

In my late 20s, I began to experience deep struggles and frustrations about being single. At times I would open my heart to a woman, but if the relationship didn't go anywhere or broke apart, I felt betrayed. I had given out personal information about myself, but the other person had walked away from it, not wanting to know more of me. Rejected again. At times, I was afraid that I might never find someone to love and that no one would ever love me.

Like me, many single adults want to develop an intimate relationship that won't fail or break up. Nearly half of all marriages end in divorce—who wants to become a part of that statistic? Some divorcees, after having tried to make their marriage work and failed, sense such a deep insecurity that they may feel incapable of developing another serious relationship.

You approach someone with subtle attempts at conversation. Instead of responding, the other person uses your remarks as an excuse to voice his or her own opinions. Two people merely talking without communicating from their hearts—a good definition of "boring." Words without a heart. You turn away, thinking, *Oh, what's the use?* and that's that. Superficial conversations at parties, clubs, work, and church leave you empty.

Sometimes you just sit at home alone, feeling unloved and unlovable, convinced that you are incapable of any type of significant relationship. Maybe you even go through the pity-party syndrome.

Recently I counseled a girl named Taylor about her longings for an intimate relationship with a man. While on a trip, she wrote to me, saying, "Unless I'm dating a man seriously, I don't feel much like a person. Oh, I know my parents and friends love me, but I want something much deeper. I see my friends walking arm in arm with their boyfriends, but all I can do is appreciate such romantic scenes from a distance. I have never experienced that closeness and joy, that electrifying oneness. I need a sense of hope and courage that someday I'll have that, too."

Losing Hope

Some singles live with a lack of hope, a feeling that an enjoyable, fulfilling, committed marital relationship is impossible. They have seen or experienced the devastation of divorce. Where can you find quality love that lasts until death separates you?

After I spoke at a conference in Washington, a man said to me, "You advocated building love on a strong foundation of commitment. But what is commitment? I have a hard time committing myself to someone for even one date! Whenever I'm on a date, I keep looking around at other women and become dissatisfied with the one I'm dating."

Often singles project their past or present failures into the future. They think, *I've had other relationships that have failed. I guess my future relationships won't last either.* So, although they have a desire to relate intimately with someone, they give up.

This was the case with Emily, a young woman who was being treated for depression and was convinced that beginning a relationship was futile.

"Why should I try to start a relationship?" she asked. "It will only fail, end, and hurt."

A Big Cover-Up

Obviously, most people don't go to Emily's extreme, but many give up on finding lasting satisfaction in relationships. They desperately want intimacy but don't know how to get it. Other singles focus on romantic, superficial relationships for all their satisfaction and fulfillment. They have read or heard that romantic, sexual love is the ultimate answer. But when they get involved in that part of the relationship, they fail to experience lasting fulfillment. They think that if romance is in their lives, they will be happy. But relationships don't work out that way. One person, even a spouse, can't fill all your needs and never was meant to.

A search for romance and sexual involvement is often a cover-up for hurt and an inability to get close to someone mentally and emotionally. Sometimes those who seek fulfillment in superficial liaisons have had painful relationships in the past:

- A potential love relationship ended in disappointment and broken dreams.

- Just when needed, a close friend rejected them or didn't care to understand.

- They were physically or sexually abused.

- Their parents were unhappily married or got divorced.

- No one at home seemed to reach out or care for them as children.

A person who has experienced these kinds of losses and hurts is less likely to reach out to others, fearful of ever being close to anyone again. In some cases, the person never learns how to have a deep relationship with someone else.

The Pain of Rejection

For many years, my friend Brad was unable to relate with anyone in a caring way. He only wanted to use other people to meet his own needs. He remembers watching television one evening at the age of nine while hearing the familiar sounds of a parental argument in the next room.

This time Brad also heard doors slam. Finally, his father marched through the living room carrying two suitcases. Brad ran to his dad, clung to him, and tried to pull him back from the door. "Get away," his dad shouted. "I've got to go. I refuse to live with your mother any longer!"

For years after his dad walked out, Brad felt only hurt and pain. He thought that if his father would leave him, other people would, too. In high school and college, Brad used women for his own selfish desires, never letting anyone get close to his sensitive heart. He never wanted to be rejected again.

A lot of years passed, but slowly Brad began to trust people again, to open himself to others whom he found to be trustworthy. He is still learning how to be intimate with others. Now over 30 years old, he has hopes of finding that certain someone with whom he can trust his whole self for a lifetime.

Alison was 47 years old when she got married. For many years, marriage never seemed desirable. Every marriage in her immediate family had been an unhappy one, some ending in divorce. Since childhood, the happiest family member she had known was an unmarried aunt. While Alison had a poor view of marriage, she did have a role model for happy single adulthood. So although friends encouraged her to marry, Alison decided to find happiness as a single person, like her aunt. Determined that she could be both single and fulfilled, she set out to prove it.

Did it work? Yes, until the right person came along. But it was after God had shown Alison many happy marriages among her Christian friends. Then she discovered that a fulfilling marriage was not only possible, but even possible for *her*. She had not been raised to know how to find fulfillment in close relationships. But over her long years of single adulthood, she did learn, through the

Lord's guidance, how to relate to and trust friends, relatives, and coworkers in ever-deepening friendships.

Alison's first priority in intimacy is now her husband, but those other significant relationships make her marriage all the more fulfilling. They fill up the areas that her marriage relationship wasn't meant to fill. They were the training ground for the deep fulfillment in love and intimacy, through being both a friend and lover to her husband, that she has found in marriage.

Intimacy Includes Risk

If love and intimacy are so fulfilling, why do so many married and single people have difficulty finding them—not just male-female love, but love between close friends of the same sex, love between siblings, love between parents and children? What is so attractive and yet so fearful about loving people? What is the difference between loving a sport, loving a car, loving a pet, or even loving God, and that kind of love between persons that deeply satisfies our hearts and souls?

The difference has to do with emotional intimacy and the risk of rejection. You don't need to worry about rejection when you love something that is as impersonal as sports or your car. Impersonal things won't turn on you or misunderstand. Only in our imaginations can a love relationship with another person be without risk of rejection and loss.

When we face reality, we know that the love of another person involves risk. C.S. Lewis describes two basic kinds of love: need-love and gift-love.[1] We need the love of others. But we also want to give love to others. Both types of love involve the danger of being rejected. The other person can accept our gift-love but refuse to love us back. In this way, he or she refuses to satisfy our need-love. The other person also can grant us need-love, but have such a sense of self-sufficiency that he or she refuses to allow us the satisfaction of gift-love.

We Need to Love and Be Loved

We all need to love and accept the love of other people. Even though we talk about being self-sufficient, we are made by God with a need to connect with others. You can be deeply involved in your job, become successful, and increase your income and status. At the same time, if you only experience loveless coexistence with others, the satisfaction you might have from your job or other endeavors is spoiled.

Why do we search for intimacy, for closeness and oneness? The answer is that we want to share ourselves with someone and to be accepted for just who we are. We are inadequate to rely totally upon ourselves. Intimacy is more than loving and being loved; it also helps us grow and develop as persons.

Desperation

At times, I desperately yearned for this type of closeness. During one cold January I became so anxious to get married that I lamented, "If I don't find a woman I want to marry by the first of September, I'm going to explode." The closer that date came, my frustration level increased. Finally, it was August 1, then August 15, and still there was no potential Mrs. Purnell on the horizon. September came and went. I felt empty and bewildered. What is the solution?

As a single person grows older, more of his or her friends drop out of the single world into marriage. This can make a person feel desperate enough to try crazy things.

I came to that point. I was scheduled to speak at a series of meetings in Dallas, Texas. About a month before my arrival, I phoned my friend Andy, who lived in the city. "Do you know a woman I could date for a big event on my day off?" He suggested we get two other couples to join us. It sounded like fun. We eagerly planned the night of nights.

When I arrived, Andy told me the woman he had in mind couldn't make it, but his girlfriend Jenny volunteered to find someone else for me. Immediately I was skeptical. I've always ended up disappointed with blind dates arranged by women. "She has a great personality" was usually the kindest thing that could be said about the arranged matchup.

My skepticism turned to horror when I discovered that Jenny didn't even know the woman she had gotten as my date. A friend of Jenny's had recommended her. The situation looked bleak indeed. To break the tension, Andy and I joked about how miserable my evening was about to become.

That night three couples and I piled into a large SUV and drove to the condominium where my blind date lived. I had everyone line up at her front door, with me standing in the back. That way, while she met the other people, I'd check her out and decide what I thought the evening was going to be like.

When the door opened, there stood an attractive blonde. Brooke, a flight attendant for a large airline company, was not only good-looking but interesting to talk with. I'm sure the other guys were jealous of me that night as Brooke and I talked and talked. I was thoroughly excited about the evening and showed it. Meanwhile, I thought, *This is it—the first time ever that a blind date has worked out for me!* I asked her for another date, but she was already tied up. Several times during the next few days I asked her out, but she was always busy. I never got the hint.

On my speaking trip the following month, I spotted Brooke in the Atlanta airport. She didn't seem to show much response to my greeting. Of course, she was busy working at the time, but it took a while for me to realize that Brooke really didn't want to go out with me again. When it finally hit me, all my dreams of dating and developing a relationship with this exciting person went out the window. I was blind to her disinterest. Some dreams die hard.

Missing the Point

Like others, I had such a desire for intimacy that just a glimmer of hope had caused me to pin all my dreams on one meeting. When it didn't work out, I crashed.

Later on, I realized I needed to learn how to develop and sustain a love relationship. I had missed the whole concept of friendship! No one ever told me! Having close friends eases the pain of the search for that potential love. Then, when that person does come along, we've already learned how to develop a lasting, fulfilling relationship. When many of our needs are met through other relationships, we will not expect that individual to meet more of our needs than one person is capable of doing. Our experience in developing closeness with our friends will make the building of a quality love relationship with a person of the opposite sex less stressful and a lot more rewarding.

This book is written to help you develop a close, exciting friendship with someone of the opposite sex that will become the basis for a lasting love.

Unfortunately, our society has changed the word "lover" to refer often to someone who sexually excites you, especially a person with whom you are not married. I prefer to define a lover as a person who has founded a quality love relationship on biblical principles—a relationship filled and overflowing with the dynamic love that only God can give a man and woman for each other.

2

The Foundation for a Lasting Love

■ ■ ■

As I travel across the country to speak to audiences, I have discovered that the primary topic people want to hear about is relationships.

Many of their questions regarding relationships can be summarized in this one question: How can I find a quality love relationship that will last?

We all look for someone to love, both romantically and as an intimate friend. Most of us want to be loved for who we are way down deep inside and to be able to share our deepest thoughts and feelings with one another.

Many people indicate that their first desire is to marry someone who is their closest friend, someone with whom they have enjoyed close companionship and with whom an emotional relationship has developed. In this way, there will be a strong foundation for a romantic relationship that is not built primarily on superficial feelings or sexual attraction. Many people truly want to be friends first.

Although this is a widely expressed desire, I have found that the ideal of being a friend first falls victim to the pull of becoming a romantic lover first. Many people who think they know how to be a lover are easily swept into the wrong kind of relationship by their emotions and passions. They grapple with how to be friends.

After I spoke about sex and the search for intimacy at a conference, Harry approached me and said, "I've been dating Leigh for several months, and we've become very close. In fact, we've made love a couple of times. I really like Leigh. But the other day her friends told me she was upset with me. When I called her, she said she didn't want to see me again. What's wrong with her?"

I had a hunch. "Maybe Leigh feels guilty about your sexual involvement," I replied. "She may even hate you."

"What do you mean?" Harry retorted. "I told her I loved her. We made love together. So why does she reject me now?"

"I don't know about your specific situation," I responded, "but sexual involvement without marriage commitment often leads to rejection. When a man violates a woman or overcomes her sexual inhibitions with his persuasiveness, she may grudgingly participate (and perhaps even end up enjoying it at the moment) but later on feel empty and guilty and eventually turn against him. Just the fact that she told her friends to tell you instead of telling you herself shows she doesn't even want to talk with you. She's angry. You became her sexual lover without ever becoming her friend."

In our desire to fill our lives with instant joy and happiness, we have overlooked the whole idea of friendship. In fact, many of the people we call friends are only acquaintances. Often people have what I call "Hi! Bye!" relationships. Someone runs in to you and says, "Hi! How are you doing?" and then walks away without waiting for an answer. In fact, he probably doesn't want an answer. When people ask you how you are doing, have you noticed how fidgety they get when you actually start to tell them? We live in a sea of superficial relationships.

The Primary Purpose of Dating

Many people have become confused about the purposes of dating. For some, it is a way to have fun and hang out with another person. But the purpose of dating is not just to have fun or to fill your social calendar. The main reason to date is more important than finding someone who is attractive and with whom you can become romantically involved.

The primary purpose of dating is to build a quality relationship with another person. You learn the similarities and differences between yourselves. You learn how to communicate and how to be vulnerable with each other. You develop common interests and grow in your understanding of the opposite sex. You learn to encourage and to give to another person. As with any human endeavor, there are problems associated with dating. But if your purpose is to develop a quality, healthy relationship, it is a good way to find out your compatibility in many areas. Dating sets the stage for marriage—either to the person you are currently dating or to someone yet to come. You form the foundation for a long-term relationship from the first date, a foundation you aren't even aware of because you don't even know if a relationship will deepen, much less lead to marriage.

When I was on the West Coast speaking at some meetings, one leader of the sponsoring group asked to talk with me privately. As we sat in Tim's car, he related a sequence of short romances. They all followed a pattern. He would meet an attractive woman and quickly begin dating her because of his loneliness and desire for intimacy. Then he would quickly become overly affectionate with her. One thing would lead to another, and he would find himself more emotionally and physically involved than he intended. He would feel guilty and empty because there was nothing to hold the relationship together except fleeting romantic feelings. After a short time, the inevitable painful breakup would occur. That day Tim asked me, "Why do I do the same things again and again? I'm constantly digging myself out of the same hollow situation."

Too often, people start off with romantic attraction, hoping that they will later become friends. But the more you become involved sexually, the less likely you are to spend quality time talking about deep, significant subjects that really matter to your lives and future happiness. Physical contact, which at first may be limited to kissing goodbye at the end of a date, ends up becoming the date. All other activities are merely time fillers in comparison to the make-out scene.

As a result, a couple often finds they have more and more arguments and misunderstandings. Eventually the relationship deteriorates because it is based on the physical and romantic rather than on a solid foundation of friendship. After a while, physical involvement becomes unfulfilling and even repulsive without lifelong commitment.

Some people feel more comfortable working at their computers or other machines than interacting with human beings. In fact, one man told me that because he works 60 to 70 hours a week programming computers, he doesn't have time to develop close friends. So he just "downloads his stuff" with a woman in a short time—he hooks up with someone for a night and goes back to work the next day. That is a formula for disaster.

Then, through present pain and memories of past failures, a person wants to know how to correct the pattern of broken relationships. The bewildering question is, How can I change? My suggestion is to start your relationship differently. Instead of allowing your passions to guide the relationship, let your mind rule over your emotions. It will not be easy, but you will build a much better foundation for a healthy and satisfying long-term relationship.

The Importance of Friendship

The ability to develop deep friendships determines the depth of emotional intimacy that we will experience in our relationships. I am not referring to mere acquaintances or people you occasionally hang out with but about friends in the real sense—people to whom you can open up your heart and life.

It comes as no surprise that the expectations in a friendship are closely linked to those in marriage. Many singles I counsel say they want a spouse who is their best friend. They express the hope of marrying someone who will be faithful, trustworthy, honest, transparent, fun, and a host of other qualities that emanate from an intimate friendship. Since those characteristics represent what they want in their ideal relationship, they must develop them before they get married. Just walking down the aisle in a marriage ceremony will not suddenly give them to you.

In the process of building an enjoyable companionship, you learn the art of good communication and mutual respect. A satisfying marriage is built on the solid foundation of loyalty, transparency, and shared interests. In dating, all of these qualities are in their rudimentary form. The development of good interpersonal skills leads to a strong, committed relationship. Perhaps this is because the ingredients that go into building deep relationships are *learned* behaviors. Being vulnerable, dealing with conflict, and remaining faithful to someone do not come automatically. We learn to be an intimate friend by developing these skills.

So how can you learn such traits as loyalty and vulnerability?

Become Friends with Others of Your Own Sex

A great place to start is with a roommate or a friend with whom you enjoy spending time. You may think these relationships are nothing like a marriage commitment. After all, if you have an argument with a friend, you can just say goodbye. In marriage, that kind of reaction isn't so easy. But if you haven't built any commitment in same-sex relationships, it's hard to develop commitment in opposite-sex relationships. If you have difficulty opening up and being vulnerable to someone of your own sex, the chances are that you will have difficulty opening up to someone of the opposite sex. You can learn to be faithful in your commitments right now. We will discuss how to develop these qualities in a later chapter.

Strong friendships with people of your own sex provide an excellent learning environment. You can develop habits and relational skills that will be essential in relationships with the opposite sex and eventually in your marriage relationship. Same-sex friendships make our lives healthy and well-rounded. No one person can meet all our emotional needs—not even a spouse. Couples who do not allow friendships outside the dating or marriage relationships end up hurting themselves. In time, through their exclusiveness, they will find themselves friendless.

Throughout my relationship with my wife, Paula, I've encouraged her to develop friendships with other women. I know that I cannot be everything Paula needs. I'm a man, and I can't take the place of a female friend. I can't communicate with her or respond to her the way another woman would. Paula needs her close friendships with other women. And I need close friendships with other men.

Become a Student of the Opposite Sex

We need practice in developing strong friendships with the opposite sex. Men and women are different in many areas. We think and relate differently. So wherever I go, I advocate that people become students of the opposite sex. Perhaps your response is, "Great! Where is a subject for me to study?" It sounds exciting, and it is, but for a reason other than what you might think. To become such a student is to learn about the intricacies of members of the opposite sex, to develop intimacy built on understanding, not on romance. A good way to do this is to become friends with someone of the opposite sex you are not interested in romantically—perhaps someone much older or younger than yourself, or a relative, or a long-term acquaintance.

Ask questions about areas that puzzle you. Seek that person's advice. Read books about the opposite sex that help you understand their concerns, needs, attitudes, and the ways they communicate.

What It Takes to Be a Friend

As you learn as much as you can about the opposite sex, keep these points in mind:

1. Communication

Communication is the lifeblood of a relationship. As long as we communicate openly and honestly, our relationship will be alive with oneness. When we begin to protect ourselves by sharing only partially, the relationship begins to deteriorate and die. A relationship is only as good as the communication within it.

You can learn step-by-step how to communicate. *First, learn to share who you are,* that is, what you think, feel, value, love, esteem, hate, fear, desire, hope for, believe in, and are committed to. When you open up and communicate these things, the other person will begin to understand who you are.

One of the benefits of being honest and vulnerable with another person is that you have an opportunity to be accepted unconditionally for who you are. As a result, you will experience something of what God's unconditional love for us is like through the relationship.

Second, learn to work through differences and conflicts. When conflict arises in a relationship (and it most certainly will at some point), you have the option of striking out, walking out, or talking it out. Talking it out develops mutual understanding of your differences and unique points of view.

In dealing with conflict, you must make a real effort to understand the other person. What are his or her feelings and thoughts, and why does he or she think that way?

Work through differences. Friends who are roommates can have all kinds of differences that need to be worked through. Sometimes they make you angry. "Why doesn't she pay her part of the monthly rent on time?" "Why doesn't he clean up the mess he made?"

The temperature of the home or office can be a strong point of disagreement. One may like it cold and the other hot. I had a roommate who loved his room ice-cold. In the winter, Brian opened the windows all the way and slept in little clothing under a thin sheet. I liked my room warm. Every night I would go to the thermostat, turn up the heat, and go back to bed. Later, Brian would sneak into the hallway and turn the thermostat down. In the middle of the night, I would wake up freezing and turn the thermostat higher. One time he tricked me by going down to the basement and turning off the furnace completely. I froze that night, but never caught on. Now we laugh about it, but at the time it raised our emotional temperatures.

Besides seeking to understand the other person and his or her viewpoint, we need to be willing to listen. Too often we are so busy thinking about when to interrupt that we fail to really hear what that person is saying. Listening is an act of recognition. It's an important part of communication that shows you care about the other person and what he or she has to say. When we listen, we can respond to what the person is saying and where he or she is coming from. Listening is being involved with the other person mentally and emotionally. It shows that we are not being preoccupied with ourselves.

2. Sacrifice and Commitment

Sacrifice and commitment are qualities you don't hear much about nowadays. Learn to sacrifice—your schedule, your time, your activities, perhaps even your belongings—for the sake of a relationship. Give-and-take is important in any human relationship and particularly in one involving commitment. For the sake of a friendship, you may decide to participate in activities that your friend enjoys rather than demanding to do only things you enjoy.

Too often we want the benefits of a deep friendship without putting in the hard work that kind of relationship requires. But we cannot have the benefits without paying the price. Intimacy and commitment go hand in hand.

In any intimate relationship, there may be times when one person will have to do most of the giving. This is the test of loyalty: the ability to look beyond our own needs and stick by our friends. A true friendship will be characterized by mutual loyalty and interdependence.

To see a relationship grow, we need to make the decision to sacrifice and commit ourselves to the other person through good and bad times. The book of Proverbs says, "A friend loves at all times, and a brother is born for adversity."[1]

3. Trust and Trustworthiness

Before we can be committed in a relationship, we need to develop trust. Faithfulness, an act of our will, is in reality the fruit of trust.

We must develop the quality of being trustworthy so people can feel safe with us and know that we will not betray or desert them. Trustworthiness also involves keeping confidences. This allows people to share inner thoughts or feelings, knowing that these will stop with us and not be broadcast any further. Without mutual trust, we have no desire to give ourselves freely and unreservedly. As a result, relationships are undermined.

Novelist George Eliot said, "Friendship is the inexpressible comfort of feeling safe with a person, having neither to weigh thoughts nor measure words. We can only do this with someone we trust."

When Jim and I roomed together in Bloomington, Indiana, we worked for different organizations. It was fun to find out what was going on in each other's life. Another guy invited me over for lunch one day. As we ate our food, this guy proceeded to criticize my work and tell me all the things he did not like about me. He had a negative attitude about his life and he was taking it out on me. I felt ambushed.

That evening I sat dejectedly in a big chair watching a game on TV. Jim walked into the room, took one look at me, and said, "What's wrong with you?"

I tried to hide my discouragement. "Oh, nothing," I replied halfheartedly.

"Hey, you look like you're sick or something. Tell me what's going on."

I bared my soul, explaining what the other guy said to me. I acted like a hurt puppy cowering in a corner somewhere. I felt as if my work and character had been maligned viciously. I hung my head down and sighed.

When I finished, Jim stood up and shouted, "He's wrong! I know you very well. And I know him. Everything he criticized about you came from his own failures. He's just jealous. Don't let his bad attitudes discourage you."

Wow! Jim lifted me up at a time when I was down. He had my heart in his hands, and he gave me courage to handle false criticism. I found that I could trust him with my inner thoughts. That strengthened our friendship.

4. Acceptance and Respect

If we are unable to accept and respect friends for who they are—their strengths and their weaknesses—then we will constantly try to change them.

Everyone has idiosyncrasies and weaknesses. If we can't accept these, then we will put tremendous pressure on both the person and the relationship. Very few relationships can withstand this type of destructive pressure.

Jesus warned us about picking each other apart. "Why do you look at the speck that is in your brother's eye, but do not notice the log that is in your own eye?... First take the log out of your own eye, and then you will see clearly to take the speck out of your brother's eye."[2]

We build respect when we put another person's faults and virtues into perspective. Then we can encourage the development of their strengths and be patient with their weaknesses. Jim did that for me.

5. Encouragement

Encouraging a friend involves being there for that person and asking God for wisdom to listen, to empathize, and to know how to respond. It involves helping your friend see his or her circumstances from God's perspective.

Encouragement involves not only what we say but what we do for someone. Running errands or taking care of other tasks for the person may relieve some of the weight pressing in on him or her. Encouragement involves time and creativity.

It means giving an honest compliment, saying the positive things about another that we often think but neglect to verbalize. Proverbs says, "Oil and perfume make the heart glad, so a man's counsel is sweet to his friend."[3]

6. Hard Work and Maintenance

Reach out to build up other people, and they will build you up. Developing good friendships is like riding a bicycle—you either go forward or you fall down. Effort and hard work are required. Relationships don't just happen. They must be nurtured and maintained. A relationship that is worth anything takes determination from both people involved.

Look for a Friend—Not a Spouse

Paula and I focused on these six components as our friendship developed into a serious dating relationship. As a result, it was my joy and privilege to marry my best friend.

A relationship is wonderfully satisfying and mutually beneficial when it is built on friendship, caring, mutual respect, and fun.

Bill, a single businessman, told me about his ups and downs in the business world. At the end of our conversation, he said that one of the major hurdles in his life was that there was no one to share his victories and defeats. Even though he had friends, he felt as if he were all alone to deal with the world. Because of all his business problems and debts, he said, "I guess no one would want to marry me. I'll be alone the rest of my life."

Personally, I believe Bill's statement is wrong. Even if he doesn't get married for a while, he could build good friendships with women he enjoys spending time with. They don't have to be potential marriage partners to be fun to be with. Many delightful women would encourage him through the ups and downs if he would take the effort to get to know them. Don't paint yourself into a corner by saying that no one is going to like you because you have problems. Instead, reach out to build up other people, and they will build you up. If you want to have a friend, be a friend.

In my 42 years of being single, I had many problems. But when I reached out to others, my problems were minimized. When I gave my life away, I found that I received so much in return and ended up with more to give away. This is the foundation for a quality relationship.

My advice to Bill was, "When you are interested in dating, don't look for someone to marry. Focus on building a good friendship."

Another man told me, "I judge women before I even get to know them. I just look at them and decide whether I'm going to like them or not." How pathetic! Unfortunately, this is a common tendency. Our eyes see what we think we want, but our eyes are often wrong. The person you label as unexciting might actually possess the characteristics that would provide an exciting relationship for you.

Paula and I found this out. We knew each other for a year before we started dating seriously. I wouldn't recommend our first date as the way to start a relationship—it was a disaster. Our second date didn't happen until nine months later. It took that long to get over our first impressions.

Finding My Lifelong Best Friend

I met Paula on a beautiful June afternoon on the campus of Colorado State University while I was teaching a course at Campus Crusade's Institute of Biblical Studies.

I was sitting in the campus medical clinic after getting an allergy shot when I saw two women come down the hall in tennis outfits.

I don't play much tennis. Racquetball is my game. But when Paula sat down next to me, suddenly tennis became my favorite sport. Soon we were discussing the finer points of the game. During our conversation, I discovered that Paula was attending the conference. But after our casual conversation I forgot her name.

Three weeks later she walked into the conference dining room. My heart skipped a beat. Nonchalantly, I just happened to meet her at the salad bar. I found out her name and later that evening asked her to go with me to a concert the following Friday. But when the date came around, another woman was on my mind, so I hardly paid attention to Paula. In fact, for nine months I didn't give her another thought.

In April I went to Florida State University for a three-night speaking series titled "Dynamic Relationships." I was surprised to learn that Paula was the associate director of the Campus Crusade ministry on the campus and was assigned to be my liaison. She drove me to all my speaking engagements.

After the speaking series ended, Paula drove me to the airport. When we stopped at a restaurant for something to eat, she asked me if I remembered our date the previous summer.

"What date?" I replied. I couldn't remember it! She reminded me of some of the things we did, including the concert we attended. I remembered doing all those things, but to this day I don't remember that she was the one I was with. Obviously, this shocked her, but she was also amused by it. She later told me that at that point, she decided I must be a real character!

At the concert that previous June, I had seen Wendy, a woman whom I had asked to go to the concert with me a week before I asked Paula. I really liked Wendy and was very disappointed when she told me she had other plans. *Why would she prefer to go out with some other guy and not with me?* My mind was fixated on the woman who had rejected me. The rest of the night I didn't say much to Paula. All I could think of was how much Wendy had hurt me.

After that date, Paula's friends asked her, "What is Dick like?"

"He's boring."

What a great way to start a relationship! She thought I was boring, and I couldn't remember her. Sitting in that restaurant in Tallahassee, Florida, nine months later, sharing honestly those first impressions of each other broke the ice for us. I couldn't believe how fickle I had been.

In the course of the conversation, I asked her what she did in her spare time. She told me she was reading *The Rise and Fall of the Third Reich.* That's a massive book. I was impressed.

After I left, I obviously had to write to Paula. All in the line of duty, of course. In the letter I asked her what else she was doing with her spare time. She wrote back that while the students were busy with their final exams, she decided to learn more about baseball. She went to a double-header and ended up sitting next to the girlfriend of one of the players. The woman explained the rules and strategy of the game to Paula.

It impressed me that Paula wanted to learn about lots of different things. That she would read a book about the Second World War and attend a doubleheader baseball game intrigued me. I didn't know her very well, but I was interested in the mystery of Paula, and I wanted to get to know her better. By this time, she was mildly interested in me also.

The next summer, at the same annual Colorado confer-ence, I decided to spend some time with her, as well as with some other women. Actually, my roommate and I had made a bet to see who would be the first to date ten dif-ferent women that summer. I wasn't looking to marry or settle down; I just wanted to have fun and enjoy getting to know the women on my Ten Most Wanted list.

At the end of two weeks, I had gotten dates with six different women. I was having fun, but I quit the contest because two of them caught my attention: Kathy and Paula. But on a Friday night date with Kathy, I realized I was miserable. Afterward I thought, *Why should I waste my time? I thoroughly enjoy being with Paula. She's a lot of fun, and I'm interested in knowing more about her.* I decided to pursue our friendship. I wasn't looking for marriage; I simply wanted to spend more time with her. Being with Paula was exciting.

After a few weeks, Paula told me, "Dick, we're spending a lot of time together, and I don't want you to get the wrong impression. I enjoy being with you, but I don't think our relationship could ever go anywhere, so maybe we should stop dating."

"Paula," I responded, "I just want to be your friend. If you don't want to date, that's okay. But I thoroughly enjoy being with you and getting to know you better."

"Really?" she said. "Do you think we can date and still be just friends?"

"Sure. I'm not interested in getting serious right now, but I am interested in building a friendship."

We continued to date, learning about each other and talking about every subject imaginable. One day Paula told her roommate some of the things we had discussed. Her roommate said, "I've been dating my boyfriend for almost two years, and we don't talk about the kind of stuff that

Dick and you discuss." Paula and I were open and honest and enjoyed getting to know each other's intricacies.

By the time we got married a year later, we were best friends. Our joy in learning about one another and wanting to have an emotional connection grew and multiplied. Instead of looking for romance, we looked for enjoyment with a friend.

Becoming a student of the opposite sex allowed each of us to develop friendships and caring relationships. Many single adults are too quick to cut off potential relationships if the person isn't a prospective spouse. Don't be too impatient to get something serious going. Relax and commit yourselves just to enjoying each other and to becoming friends.

I lost the bet with my roommate that summer, but I gained a permanent best friend.

A Balanced Relationship Star

■ ■ ■

3

Components of
Oneness

■ ■ ■

When Jessica first moved to Chicago, it seemed that people were always asking her if she knew Nick. She was lonely and wanted to get to know people. She spotted Nick at an office party and was attracted to him immediately. She must have been staring at him because a coworker asked her, "Do you know Nick?"

"No," Jessica replied, "but I sure would like to." The coworker introduced them, and in a few weeks, Nick asked her for a date.

During that first date, she returned from the restaurant ladies' room to find Nick entertaining a group of people with his antics. She was watching with the rest of the crowd when another girl asked her, "Do you know that funny guy?"

"Yes, a little," Jessica said, somewhat embarrassed. "He's my date."

Getting to know Nick better became a regular thing. Many dates and a year later, Jessica and Nick celebrated their engagement at a very nice restaurant overlooking a lake. When Jessica stepped away from their table for a few moments and then returned, she found Nick joking with the people around him as usual. As she approached, a waitress asked her if she knew the guy who was keeping his end of the restaurant entertained. Used to Nick's antics by then and no longer flustered by them, she answered, "Oh, I know him pretty well. He's my fiancé."

Six months later, at the rehearsal dinner for their wedding, a childhood friend of Nick's started teasing Jessica. "Do you really know this crazy guy you're marrying?" he said. "If you did, I'm sure you'd think twice about getting yourself tied to this nut!"

Laughing at his teasing, Jessica said, "You bet I know him. That's why I'm marrying him."

Having been asked the question so many times during their courtship, Jessica started thinking about it more seriously. *Do I really know Nick?* Well, if not, she knew she would once they were married.

As the years went by, Jessica often thought about that question. Did she really know who Nick was? Each year she could say she knew him better than the year before. At the same time, she would always ask herself, "But do I really, truly know him? How long will that take?"

How long? That question can be partially answered by something my dad told me one day. After 41 years of marriage, my father admitted to me, "Dick, sometimes I still don't understand your mother!"

To know a person takes a lifetime of working at a relationship. Intimacy doesn't happen overnight or even after several months of dating.

The dictionary defines intimacy as a close personal relationship marked by affection, love, and knowledge of each other's inner character, essential nature, and innermost true self; complete intermixture, compounding and interweaving.

The Real Meaning of Intimacy

Over the years, the meaning of the word "intimacy" has taken on a primarily sexual connotation. In fact, the secondary meaning of the word in some dictionaries refers to an illicit sexual affair. So today, if a person says he or she is intimate with someone of the opposite sex, most people assume the two are having sexual relations.

I prefer to define true intimacy as total life sharing—sharing your life completely with someone else. It includes being open to and deeply involved in the full life of another person, seeking to understand all that makes up that person. Intimacy is a process, not a once-and-for-all accomplishment. Each of us is developing, growing, learning, and aging throughout our lives. Life is in constant flux, so healthy intimacy is not static. Learning about someone you love is an exciting adventure that can last a lifetime. Any couple who says that their relationship is boring has probably stopped growing in their oneness and started drifting apart.

The five major areas of a person's life are the social, emotional, mental, physical, and spiritual. These can be represented graphically by a five-pointed star. Knowing only one or two of these areas of another person's makeup creates a very superficial impression of who that person is. To be intimate with someone, we must share the joys and sorrows, the ups and downs, the likes and dislikes, and the strengths and weaknesses in each of these areas. In this way we can know each other as we really are. Mutually caring, giving, and accepting each other, we grow to both understand and love.

Each of us possesses our own personal star. Growing in all five areas at the same time is a difficult task, if not impossible. We seem to be able to handle two or maybe three areas at a time but not all five together. We are always trying to put our life in order—"to get our ducks in a row." But one or more of the ducks always seem to be swimming out of line. This drift brings disorder and confusion.

When two people become interested in each other and begin to seriously develop a relationship, they are actually trying to get their individual stars in alignment with each other. They form a Relationship Star. Forming this Relationship Star will help them build an enjoyable friendship and experience a wonderful sense of togetherness.

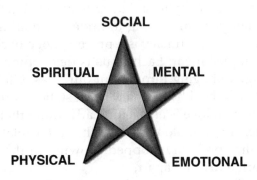

Singles often ask me the significant question, How can I know if a certain person is the right one for me? That is a simple question, but the answer is complicated. Part of my answer relates to the Relationship Star. Do the five major areas of your lives form a clear Relationship Star. Do you have a growing desire to know each other more completely in each the five areas?

By using the Relationship Star as a guide, you will be able to evaluate your friendship and decide whether to pursue a deeper relationship.

Let's start with an evaluation that you can measure. Take a few minutes to reflect on the extent of your relationship by taking the "Friends and More" Quiz. Indicate your responses on a scale of one to five. One means "no," three is a neutral reply, and five means "yes." Ask the person you are interested in to take the quiz, too, with your friendship in mind. Compare your answers. It is a simple tool to help you analyze how both of you feel about each other. How well do you really understand each other? Do you both genuinely desire to progress forward, or is one more interested than the other?

Friends and More

The Social Area

Do you enjoy going to public events together?

   1   2   3   4   5

Do you enjoy doing activities together?

   1   2   3   4   5

Do you agree on how you each spend money?

   1   2   3   4   5

Do you appreciate each other's work ethic?

   1   2   3   4   5

Do you have a good rapport with each other's family?

   1   2   3   4   5

Do you know and approve of each other's friends?

   1   2   3   4   5

Do you encourage each other to meet new people?

   1   2   3   4   5

Do you appreciate each other's social habits?

   1   2   3   4   5

Do your friends encourage your friendship?

1 2 3 4 5

Do you agree about punctuality and the use of time?

1 2 3 4 5

The Emotional Area

Do you really try to understand each other?

1 2 3 4 5

Do you communicate well?

1 2 3 4 5

Do you listen attentively to each other as you share your fears, joys, ambitions, failures, hopes?

1 2 3 4 5

Do you share each other's concerns?

1 2 3 4 5

Do you have habits that upset each other?

1 2 3 4 5

Do you share joyful and painful experiences?

1 2 3 4 5

Are you comfortable with the way you each react (both positively and negatively) to significant circumstances?

1 2 3 4 5

Do you have shared interests?

1 2 3 4 5

Do you each apologize for hurtful statements and mis-understandings?

1   2   3   4   5

The Mental Area

Do you know each other very well?

1   2   3   4   5

Do you agree about roles and responsibilities in marriage?

1   2   3   4   5

Do you make difficult decisions together?

1   2   3   4   5

Do you adjust to and compromise with each other when you have differences?

1   2   3   4   5

Do you have similar attitudes about family life and children?

1   2   3   4   5

Do you appreciate each other's sense of humor?

1   2   3   4   5

Do you discuss politics, national issues, and current events?

1   2   3   4   5

Is each of you humble when you are right and teachable when you are wrong?

1   2   3   4   5

Do you share similar levels of educational and work experience?

1   2   3   4   5

Do you both continue to learn new things and grow intellectually?

1   2   3   4   5

The Physical Area

Do you appreciate each other's appearance?

1   2   3   4   5

Do you like each other's style of clothes?

1   2   3   4   5

Do you respect each other's sexual boundaries?

1   2   3   4   5

Do you agree on the nature of romance?

1   2   3   4   5

Do you control your passions?

1   2   3   4   5

Do you agree about the importance of personal physical fitness?

1   2   3   4   5

Does each of you enjoy sports and participate in them?

1   2   3   4   5

Does each of you keep up your physical well-being?

1   2   3   4   5

Do you share a similar level of energy and drive?

1   2   3   4   5

The Spiritual Area

Do you share similar religious and spiritual convictions?

1   2   3   4   5

Do the spiritual beliefs each of you hold affect your daily living?

1   2   3   4   5

Does each of you have a personal faith in God?

1   2   3   4   5

Do you share a similar understanding about the death and resurrection of Christ?

1   2   3   4   5

Do your attitudes about the Bible agree?

1   2   3   4   5

Do both of you pray reguarly?

1   2   3   4   5

Do you both study the Bible?

1   2   3   4   5

Can you support and encourage each other's spiritual gifts?

1   2   3   4   5

Have you talked about eternal life?

1   2   3   4   5

Does each of you share your faith with others?

1   2   3   4   5

These questions will give you an objective assessment of your relationship and help you discuss your similarities and differences. They give you insight into the depth of your knowledge and understanding of each other. They are interrelated and will give you a fuller picture of your friendship.

As you progress in your knowledge of and experience with each other, you will recognize the necessity for a mutual foundation and set of guidelines for developing harmony and intimacy in your relationship.

A Lopsided Star

When a greater importance is placed on one or two aspects of our five-pointed Relationship Star, the relationship becomes unbalanced and results in frustration.

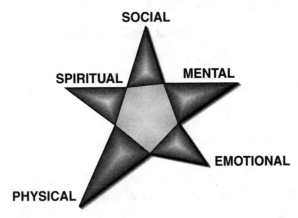

Physical Overemphasis

Overemphasis in the physical area usually results from a couple becoming too romantically involved. They may engage in inappropriate physical touching and stimulation. Their activity may even go so far as premarital intercourse. Such physical behavior affects the other areas negatively. In the emotional area, it produces guilt, fear, anger, or rejection. In the spiritual area, one grows cold toward God. You don't want to be around Christians who love God if you are guilt-ridden about your sexual activities. Praying about your relationship is difficult. Because you feel guilty, you may be afraid that God will take the person away from you.

In the mental area, thinking about the other person is always focused on the physical. You plan the date hoping to end up making out. Because you don't know the person well in the other areas of his or her life, gnawing questions arise: *Does my lover love me just for my looks? For my body? For sex? How can my lover really love me for who I am? He (she) doesn't really know who I am!*

Social Overemphasis

Overemphasis on the social area of a relationship usually means that a couple puts on a happy face in public but cannot get along in private. Their friends may tell them, "You look so good and so right together." This becomes a subtle pressure to stay together even though they can't get along and are still undeveloped in other areas of their relationship.

Social overemphasis affects the emotions. Without a growing harmony, arguments can erupt. One or both feel insecure about the stability of the relationship. When one is talking with another person or even looking at someone else, the other is jealous and angry.

Overemphasis on the social often drives a couple to become physically involved when they are in private because they have little else to enjoy when they are alone together. If one of them has convictions about too much physical involvement, he or she may try to arrange for them to be alone together as little as possible.

Cindy and Dan are an example. They were a good-looking couple, particularly at church. They enjoyed tennis, movies, parties, and concerts. In none of these activities did they have to relate intimately one-on-one, which was fine with Dan. Other than their public activities, he felt they really had few subjects of interest in common. Besides, Cindy had personal habits that irked him.

Cindy was a wonderful date but not someone Dan wanted to marry. He felt he could keep dating her for years—after all, they did have fun in a crowd. And during the little time they spent by themselves, Cindy was physically affectionate. Other than romantic teasing, however, they said little of substance to one another in private. But on this basis, dating Cindy was fun. It was also easier to keep dating her than to break it off and try to find someone else.

Finally, Dan saw that she was expecting that something more permanent might work out in the future. He knew then that he had to stop the relationship. They broke up, but there was bitterness on both sides. Dan and Cindy had fooled themselves, accepting fun and adventure but neglecting oneness in the other areas of their relationship.

Spiritual Overemphasis

The spiritual aspect of a relationship can be overemphasized, too. According to the old saying, "You can become so heavenly minded that you're no earthly good." A couple may emphasize seeking the Lord's guidance and Bible reading to the exclusion of becoming friends and developing common interests. When disagreements arise, they may blame them on Satan rather than recognizing that they have expectations and values that conflict. A couple should consider their differences when determining whether God has intended them for each other.

The attitude of spiritualizing everything when considering a potential spouse causes some couples to end up with acrimonious marriages. An excellent marriage is made up of two people who are good friends and good lovers. It is built on friendship and a Christ-centered oneness. Making God the center of your relationship is essential, but don't spiritualize everything to the neglect of recognizing and adjusting to your own particular differences.

Mental Overemphasis

And what might mental overemphasis be? Well, it's fun to talk about all kinds of subjects. When you first begin to date, you realize you are curious to know all you can about the other person. This is healthy and good. But don't use this curiosity to overlook the other dimensions of a relationship.

At the conclusion of a conference which I conduct for singles, a man followed me out of the auditorium. "Excuse me," he said, "I need to get some advice about my girlfriend. We have a lot of common interests and can talk about different subjects for hours. We have a great time together. We are headed toward marriage. But my main problem is that I'm not physically attracted to her. She doesn't excite me. We are good friends, but not potential lovers. Should we get married?"

I couldn't give him a definite yes or no. But I did caution him. "If you marry someone but have little desire to be romantic and express your love sexually, then your marriage will be headed for catastrophe."

Emotional Overemphasis

An overemphasis on emotions often involves feelings of romance so overwhelming that one is blinded to any potential problems in other areas. A Christian may mistake exhilarating emotions for the leading of the Spirit. But is it your natural spirit or the Holy Spirit that is leading you? When you allow your emotions to rule your head and your walk with God, basic differences between a man and a woman can be considered unimportant. Insignificant areas of agreement may seem like important "signs from the Lord" on the rightness of your relationship.

You can become so enthralled with a person that you overlook warning signs that he or she may not be the right one for you. Jackie was 27 when she met Larry, a law student, at a single-adult meeting sponsored by their church. Soon he was paying a great deal of attention to her and attending the meetings regularly.

Larry was handsome with an attractive personality, and Jackie fell head over heels in love with him. In just a couple of months they announced their engagement. Everyone was happy for them. They were an attractive couple who looked as if they would develop a model marriage.

However, one person was not sure about the relationship. Jackie's roommate thought the romance had been too fast, too furious, and too physically involved. When Jackie was around Larry, she seemed to lose her emotional balance entirely. And why, her roommate wondered, was no one sure if Larry really was a committed Christian? But everyone else was so positive toward him that she felt her questions might seem petty and make people think she was jealous.

On the day of the wedding, the congregation waited and waited for the ceremony to begin. Finally, the minister came to the front and said that the bride had collapsed and had to be taken to the hospital. Everyone thought that it was merely nerves, prewedding jitters. The following day, Larry got the hospital chaplain to perform the wedding ceremony in the hospital room. The next day, against the wishes of her doctor, Larry signed Jackie out of the hospital, and they left for the Midwest for their honeymoon and a new home.

Once he was back in law school, Larry soon found his studies kept him too busy for Christian friends. Soon he insisted that they start attending another church nearer their new home, one that was more socially prominent. He insisted they spend most of their social time with his old drinking buddies. He wanted Jackie, who did not drink alcohol, to take an active part in their raucous times. When she tried to read her Bible in the mornings, he became sullen and eventually angry.

Larry was possessed with a desire to become a politician. He certainly had the ability to get people to like him. When he first became involved with Jackie's Christian group, he thoroughly enjoyed being around such upbeat people and wanted to be accepted as one of them. As always, he had no trouble adopting the enthusiasm and language of a new group. His attraction to Jackie made him want to be a part even more. She met his criteria for a wife—beautiful and intelligent. He felt that she would make a good vote-getter in his political campaigns.

After the wedding, he focused back onto his original goal of politics. He felt he needed the support of his old friends in law school to help him on the road to a successful legal and political career. When Larry found that his efforts to manipulate Jackie into becoming the political wife he wanted had failed, he became interested in other women. Nine months after their wedding, on the verge of a nervous breakdown, Jackie left her husband and returned to her parents' home.

Jackie had let her emotions and romantic desires drown out the doubts and questions that she had about Larry. The internal stress manifested itself in stomach pains and an attack of nerves on her wedding day. Even then, she refused to recognize her underlying uneasiness. Her roommate told her what was happening. But, looking back on the situation, Jackie admitted that, at the time, she was so captivated by Larry that she did not listen to anyone.

Like many other singles, Jackie was in love with love—in love with the whole concept of being married. One can enjoy the euphoria of emotions but refuse to accept wise counsel from friends or to admit to God that the person you are dating may not be the right one. Breaking off this kind of a relationship means loneliness again and the embarrassment of admitting to friends and relatives that a wrong relationship has gone too far.

A Balanced Star

A lopsided star doesn't look right. In the same way, a lopsided relationship is unbalanced and will falter when one of its undeveloped areas is pressured. The weak areas will create stress and disunity in the relationship.

Sharing your whole life means getting your star in shape. To last a lifetime, a relationship must develop harmony, understanding, and oneness in every area of life.

Even if you aren't dating anyone seriously at present, learn to develop the ingredients of a balanced close friendship in your associations with the opposite sex. Having strong, healthy friendships is good for several reasons:

1. to understand and develop the ability to share yourself with someone else

2. to give a broadened and balanced perspective of committed companionship

3. to bring enjoyment to your single years

Oneness

The Bible gives eternal principles of living to help relationships be successful and fulfilling. The apostle Paul, through the inspiration of the Holy Spirit of God, lists some components of oneness in Philippians 2:1-2. Even though these were given to help the Philippian church achieve unity, they can also be indicators of the health of a friendship, dating relationship, or marriage. As you study these qualities, consider your close relationships. How do they compare with this biblical pattern?

If some key areas have not been developed and show little hope for doing so, you may need to reconsider whether you should continue dating a particular person. On the other hand, if these qualities are growing in both of you, you may be motivated to pursue a closer relationship. Discuss your strengths and weaknesses, and develop a plan to deepen your relationship.

Therefore if there is any encouragement in Christ,

if there is any consolation of love,

if there is any fellowship of the Spirit,

if any affection and compassion,

make my joy complete by being of the same mind,

maintaining the same love,

united in spirit,

intent on one purpose.[1]

Let's look at the components of oneness that God reveals in these verses.

1. Encouragement in Christ

True intimacy starts with oneness with Christ. A relationship with the risen Savior brings His love, power, and wisdom into your life. Only Christ can bring a change of heart and give strength to live His principles each day. The words "in Christ" occur 133 times in the books of the Bible written by the apostle Paul. To understand the importance of this term is to unlock the mysteries of our relationship with God.

The word "in" means "within the sphere of." An empty bottle thrown into the ocean is soon surrounded and filled by—within the sphere of—the entire ocean. In the same way, a person can be filled and surrounded by Christ in all His greatness. This relationship with Him is established by relying totally on the Lord for salvation and power for daily living. Without Him, we have only our frail human resources to meet the challenges of achieving happiness, satisfaction, and fulfillment.

Encouragement means to inspire with courage. As one of you faces difficulties, the other will offer a spirit of hope. You face challenges together so that when one is weak, the other can be strong in Christ's strength. If both you and your friend have a commitment to Christ and a deep desire to obey Him in everything, you will be able to inspire one another in life's toughest spots.

2. Consolation of Love

When failure, pain, tragedy, or disappointment strikes, friends need tenderness and comfort from each other. Consolation helps alleviate grief or a sense of loss.

When there are difficult times, the consolation of love empathizes with and builds up the other person. Consolation does not always involve giving an answer. Many situations have no immediate or obvious answer. At those times, consolation involves just listening as another pours out his or her thoughts and feelings.

For instance, Lenny broke his back a short while ago and was in the hospital for more than a week. The woman he dates visited him to give encouragement and comfort. When he talked about his fears concerning his rehab and potential job layoff, she listened empathetically and offered good insights and practical suggestions that helped him through the tragedy. She helped him to entrust his life and future into the comforting arms of the Savior. In his time of weakness and need, she showed herself to be a good friend.

3. Fellowship of the Spirit

Contrary to the opinions of some people, Christian fellowship is not merely drinking coffee together and talking about the weather or the latest sports events. It is sharing a communion of hearts that have been brought together by the Holy Spirit. When we become Christians, the Holy Spirit within us gives us power to live a fulfilling life and gives us oneness—fellowship of the Spirit—with one another.

This is one reason why the Bible cautions against a heart commitment to an unbeliever. When you try to become one with someone who has not received new life by the Holy Spirit, you will be frustrated. You look at life differently—one from a Christ-centered view and the other from a self-centered view. You can't become one with that person without turning cold toward the Holy Spirit.

As the apostle Paul said,

> Do not be bound together with unbelievers; for what partnership have righteousness and lawlessness, or what fellowship has light with darkness? Or what harmony has Christ with Belial [a false god], or what has a believer in common with an unbeliever?[2]

These verses apply to close relationships that involve interdependency. Even if one person is a Christian but is more committed to self, to things, or to anything other than the Lord, this uneven relationship will cause the more spiritual person to stumble.

4. Affection and Compassion

Together, affection and compassion demonstrate tenderness toward another person. Affection is a bond of caring and closeness that does not involve romantic feelings. Compassion is mercy extending itself to sympathize with another person's concerns. Compassion wants to alleviate distress. Affection and compassion see problems and reach out to try to solve them.

Christ got out of a boat and turned to see the masses of people flocking after Him. "When Jesus went ashore, He saw a large crowd, and He felt compassion for them because they were like sheep without a shepherd; and He began to teach them many things."[3] Matthew's account of the same incident adds that Jesus "felt compassion for them, and healed their sick."[4]

When the Lord saw needs, He was motivated by affection and compassion to take the necessary steps to remedy the problems. If we have experienced the ultimate solution for our own needs by relying upon the Good Shepherd, He will motivate us to show affection and compassion to others.

5. Being of the Same Mind

To be like-minded doesn't mean that two people think the same thoughts. Being of the same mind means they experience harmony in the midst of differences. Expressing opinions and speaking your mind honestly is always important. How you handle differences shows whether you are like-minded. If you and the person you are dating are constantly arguing or giving each other the silent treatment, you are not experiencing unity. Your deep desire for mental and emotional oneness is being frustrated.

Two people of like mind can relate intimately even though each one is a unique individual. They can find strength and oneness in their diversity.

6. Maintaining the Same Love

Falling in love takes little effort. The emotions seem to flow like a waterfall. But maintaining love takes work and commitment. Loving is easy when an atmosphere of romance envelops you. But when things are going wrong and romantic feelings are at zero or below, keeping love healthy requires effort.

When Paula and I bought our home in Dallas, the lawn looked beautiful and green. I mowed and watered it regularly. But once I started my speaking schedule, we were out of town a lot. The lawn was neglected. Soon weeds and crabgrass popped up through the beautiful lawn. Then ugly brown spots appeared and even uglier bugs infested the grass. A good lawn in Dallas demands constant attention and action. It took lots of effort, time, and sweat to bring our lawn back to life again. How much easier it would have been had we been able to give it regular attention all along.

Maintenance is the lifeblood of love. A couple must overcome the forces that pull people apart and cause love to become weak and die. In my book *Building a Relationship That Lasts,* I explain the five major causes for the decline of a relationship (communication gaps, unrealistic expectations, low self-image, selfishness, and sexual burnout) and how to overcome them.

To prevent these threats from destroying your relationship, both of you must be committed to developing, strengthening, and increasing your love. If you are not, a breakup is likely.

7. United in Spirit

The word "spirit" refers to the deep-down-inside you. To be united in spirit is to experience the union of your beings. You are woven together in your affection and in your commitment. You determine that nothing will separate you.

To be united in spirit in a romantic relationship involves infinitely more than just feelings. You are in touch with each other's inner character. No pretenses or facades exist. No dating games are played. Soul with soul form a single unit.

Separate individuals are brought together by God and become "united in spirit." Then, when this results in marriage, they are made into "one flesh."

8. Intent on One Purpose

Two people in an intimate association come from different backgrounds and different paths of life with different strengths and weaknesses, different personalities, different experiences, and different parents. But slowly, their paths converge into one. Each continues to possess his or her own uniqueness, but both find a harmony of direction toward the same goals in life.

Purpose in life includes much more than occupation, possessions, status, family, and friendships. It involves a basic motivation for being alive and on this earth. The apostle Paul encouraged the Christians of Rome to have the same purpose:

> Now may the God who gives perseverance and encouragement grant you to be of the same mind with one another according to Christ Jesus; that with one accord you may with one voice glorify the God and Father of our Lord Jesus Christ.[5]

You will experience a beautiful oneness when you both honestly say, "Together, we want our lives and thoughts to reflect to the world our dependence on God." If only one has this motivation, there will be discord, no matter how much you love each other. This basic issue of life must be settled.

Humility

The qualities in this list of components for oneness in Philippians are wonderful goals, but they are difficult to achieve without a catalyst—a substance that causes two or more chemicals to react together. The content of the next two verses in Philippians energizes the components into action. What is this powerful catalyst? Read the verses to discover it.

> Do nothing from selfishness or empty conceit, but with humility of mind regard one another as more important than yourselves; do not merely look out for your own personal interests, but also for the interests of others.[6]

There it is. The catalyst is humility. A humble attitude makes oneness possible. It removes arrogance and malice. Without it, you try to construct a relationship where you can be in control. When a person constantly thinks about what he or she is getting from a relationship, that person is acting selfishly and self-centeredly. It becomes hard to relax, to let go and enjoy the other person. A selfish attitude destroys oneness and leads to isolation.

Some people demand their rights, which produces hurt feelings and barriers. Self-centered pride causes problems by manipulating the other person for selfish gain. You cannot control another person and still have a sense of wholeness about yourself or about the relationship.

Instead of considering what is best for ourselves, we are to regard others as more important than ourselves. This may be hard to do, but it is rewarding.

Christ is the ultimate example of humility. In Philippians 2:5-11, the verses immediately following Paul's explanation of humility, Paul explains Christ's sacrificial attitudes and actions toward us. He includes this statement:

> Your attitude should be the same as that of Christ Jesus: Who, being in very nature God, did not consider equality with God something to be grasped, but made himself nothing, taking the

very nature of a servant, being made in human likeness. And being found in appearance as a man, he humbled himself and became obedient to death—even death on a cross![7]

That is humility and compassionate love. Because Christ gave Himself for us to serve us and meet our deepest needs, we respond by giving our lives back to Him. That is the way humility works.

To be humble doesn't mean you become a doormat for someone to walk all over your feelings and to use you. Christ humbled Himself to lay down His life for us, yet He was strong enough to stand for truth and righteousness. People did not run His life.

As you build an intimate association under Christ's influence, you will develop these components of oneness. As He draws two people together, they can build these qualities stronger and bring balance to the five main areas of life. And, along the way, the exploring, developing, growing, and discovering with each other are filled with fun and adventure.

The prospect of marriage is put in a much more balanced view when you have close, enjoyable friendships. Then marriage is not looked to as the only way to enjoy companionship and to share yourself with someone else.

The next five chapters discuss the five major areas of life and relationships at length and give practical suggestions for building intimacy and togetherness. As you read them, consider how you can form a balanced Relationship Star.

4

Your Social Life: Having Real Fun

■ ■ ■

The
SOCIAL

Do you have a light fixture in your home that is controlled by a dimmer switch? You can turn the lights
on low, then slowly turn the dimmer switch and watch the
lights get brighter and brighter. Whether your understanding
of the opposite sex is pitch dark or brilliant as sunlight,
perhaps I can help you turn up the dimmer switch.

The French say it beautifully with *vive la différence*—long
live the difference. Men and women are different. One of the
clearest indications I've seen of a genuine, deep difference
between men and women occurred when I was the director
of the Campus Crusade for Christ ministry at the University
of Georgia, where I had three women on my team.

As I was growing up, I had two brothers but no sisters.
Consequently, relating to women was a bit of a mystery to
me. I was in my late 20s, single, and unenlightened as to the
ways of women.

One day, traveling back to my home in Athens, Georgia, I saw some beautiful wildflowers along the roadside. I stopped and picked about 20. After getting back in town, I wondered what to do with them. I didn't own a vase to put them in, so I decided to take the bouquet to the women of our team, who all happened to live together.

When I knocked on the door of their apartment, Carolyn opened it. I casually explained that I had seen some wildflowers alongside the road and had picked a bouquet of them. When I asked Carolyn if she and the other women would like to have them, I was met with immediate exuberance. "Flowers? Real flowers? For us?"

Taken aback, I stammered, "They're nothing special!"

Ignoring my reply, she called to her two roommates who came running. "Look, everyone, Dick just brought us flowers!"

"Please come in," they all said excitedly.

No one could have been more welcomed by those women that day than I was with that handful of flowers. I got the royal treatment. When I left their apartment, I had absolutely no doubt that women and men look at life differently, particularly when it comes to simple things like flowers.

Living Life to the Fullest

My reason for including the differences between men and women in our discussion of dating is not to give you all the latest ideas about how to get married. I present these differences in order to help you understand and enjoy the opposite sex so that you can develop healthy relationships while still single.

I was single for 42 years of my life, and during much of that time, I wanted to get married. At times, I thought I never would. At other times, while dating certain women, I hoped I wouldn't!

As a single, I saw that many other single people were wasting their lives, waiting for the right person to come along. Then and only then did they think they would start enjoying life. I believe in living life to the fullest where you are right now. The Bible never says that marriage makes you happy. It says over and over again that God can fill our lives with love, joy, and peace.

Obviously, we need to relate to one another, enjoy each other, and function as members of the body of Christ. If what I share about relationships that last leads to marriage, fine. If it doesn't, fine. I want to help you experience all that God has for you right now and to encourage you to let Him take care of your future.

Right Attitudes About Right Relationships

No matter what your situation, attitudes toward the opposite sex are important. You may be attracted to them in general or just to some individuals who you think are very special. On the other hand, members of the opposite sex may puzzle you. You may be attracted to them but unable to figure them out. Just when you think you finally understand them, they do something that totally puzzles you.

You may be intimidated by the opposite sex. Perhaps you feel confident in your job or sports activities but feel insecure developing a close relationship. You may feel distrustful of the opposite sex. You may have been hurt in a failed marriage or broken dating relationship. You may have had great expectations and dreams that were smashed.

Perhaps promises were made to you and then broken. Maybe you exposed your heart and then found it betrayed. Whatever your painful experiences in past relationships, you can overcome the scars and develop intimacy in the social area of your star.

Through the years, I felt very confident in many areas, including my chosen profession. But in relationships with women, I felt very intimidated. Many times, I would like a woman very much but just would not know how to communicate with her. I could talk to everyone else except the one I wanted to talk to most. Through all my dating and relating, I have learned some principles that have helped me to understanding the opposite sex.

Treat a Woman Like a Woman

I personally believe that one of the greatest desires of a woman's heart is to be truly loved by one man. A woman will often say that a man is special to her or that she wants to be special to someone. While on a date with an attractive man, a woman may hope that she sparks in him a genuine interest for her.

A woman wants to feel that the man interested in her cares. The saying "Little things mean a lot" opens the door to a woman's heart. This presents a problem to many men who go along in life oblivious to little kindnesses and courtesies.

I was at a large conference in Philadelphia where my friend and former college roommate Josh McDowell was to speak. Close to midnight the night before his scheduled men's seminar on sex and dating, he called me into his room and said, "Dick, I'm really sick. I don't think I can speak tomorrow. Why don't you take my place?"

I accepted the invitation. *But what will I talk about?* was my immediate thought. As soon as I left his room, I called my girlfriend and said, "I'll be speaking to 500 men tomorrow morning about women. If you had that opportunity, what would you say to them?"

Without hesitation, she said, "I would tell them to treat a woman like a woman."

I wasn't sure that I had understood her, so later in our conversation I said, "Tell me again, what would you tell these men?"

She repeated the same words. "Treat a woman like a woman." After we hung up, I wondered what she meant. How do you treat a woman like a woman? I stayed up much of the night trying to incorporate her ideas into my speech.

Several months later I conducted a conference for singles at a large church in Houston. One participant asked me, "How do you feel about men who treat a woman like a buddy? The non-Christian men at work treat me like a lady, but Christian men treat me like I'm one of the guys. I don't want to pursue a relationship with any of the non-Christians because they want sex by the second date. But the Christian men I know aren't interested in dating me, so what do I do?"

By the end of this book, I hope I will have answered that question. But right here I urge the men to open their eyes. Women don't want to be treated like a buddy. Even if a man isn't personally interested in the women in his circle of acquaintances, he ought to treat them differently than he would the guys. Don't take a woman for granted. For instance, if a woman you know does something well, why not tell her? Let her know that you appreciate what she did and her gracious thoughtfulness. Be a source of genuine encouragement to a woman by verbalizing your positive thoughts.

How to Ask for a Date

If you are interested in asking a woman for a date, remember that she wants to feel special. Don't say, "Hi! What are you doing Friday night?" A man asks that way because he doesn't want to hear "I have other plans." He likes to cover all his bases first. He can be pretty sneaky in doing this. He tries to find out subtly from her or her friends if she is dating anyone and what her plans are for that weekend. After learning this, then he asks the question as casually as possible. Men don't like to be rejected.

The problem is that this leaves the woman in a very insecure position. It's hard for her to know how to respond to that question. If she likes the man, she doesn't want to appear anxious and say, "I'm not doing anything! What do you have in mind?" After all, what if he should say, "Oh, nothing," and then just walk away? That would be very embarrassing!

Plan ahead. A man needs to consider what he thinks a woman might like to do on a date. Then he should ask her a definite question. "Hey, there's a great concert coming up Friday night. Would you like to go to dinner and the concert with me?" She can then give a definite reply without revealing whether she's more interested in going out with him or in going to the concert. There's time to decide that later.

Even if a man starts a relationship by asking for specific dates, later on it's easy for him to slide into a rut in date-planning. After dating a particular woman awhile, too many men just say, "Well, what do you want to do Friday night?"

Then the woman will reply, "I don't know. What would you like to do?"

And the guy will come back with, "I don't know. What do you think?" Many women have told me how exasperated they become with a man's indecisiveness.

After a man has been dating a woman for a while, he should have plenty of ideas of what she likes and doesn't like to do. Together, evaluate your past dates. Ask her which ones she enjoyed the most and why. She will probably appreciate your thoughtfulness. Find out her favorites and plan some fun times in the future. Don't overlook the little things that mean a lot to her.

For instance, when my wife, Paula, was pregnant, she needed to walk every day for exercise. So, whenever she was ready, I would drop what I was doing and walk with her. After the baby was born, she told me, "Dick, I know that you truly love me."

"Really?" I said. "How do you know that?"

"Because you walked with me every day, even when I knew you didn't always want to do it."

It's the little things that say, "I love you."

Respect a Man

On the other hand, a man usually wants to be respected. Obviously, women want to be respected as well, and men want to be loved. However, a man wants to be respected by others, especially the woman he loves. A woman is surprised that a man wants to be respected above all else. A man thinks that if he can gain other people's respect, then a woman will love him. Of course, this attitude may not always work well. The man may work hard at his job, his sports interests, or some other activity trying to beat the competition and gain respect, only to end up losing his wife or girlfriend because he didn't pay enough attention to her needs. Men have a hard time learning that respect doesn't automatically carry over into love. The way to the top may not be the path to her heart.

For instance, when I started speaking nationally, I was dating a woman back home in Indiana. One day she told me that she didn't want to date me anymore. I was shocked. I said, "Come on, you really want to break up with me?" Although I didn't say it out loud, I was thinking, *Do you really know who you are dating?*

She wasn't impressed with my position. What she wanted was caring commitment, and I hadn't given her that. My busyness and insensitivity turned her off.

Men have an interesting attitude. "Look at how successful I am; look at my accomplishments. You should love me because I'm respected by others." A man hasn't learned that receiving the respect of others doesn't keep a woman's love. As a responder, a woman is more likely to love you when you show her genuine love first.

The Bible says that a man should love his wife.[1] That is translated by a woman to mean that her man makes loving her a top priority. The Bible also says that a woman should respect her husband.[2] A woman may love a man, but will she be responsive to his leading? She will be responsive if she respects and admires him, first of all for who he really is, only secondarily (and maybe not at all) for what he does. For a woman, respect can easily be the beginning of love for a man. As the man demonstrates his love for her in a multitude of ways, the woman's respect for who he really is will grow and blossom.

How can a woman begin to build respect for a man and then show him this respect? One way is to discover his strengths and encourage him to develop those strengths. Another way is to show him that she really believes in him. When he faces a big challenge, a man loves to hear a woman confidently say, "I respect you, I believe in you, and I know you can succeed."

How to Refuse a Date

Even if a woman isn't interested in dating a certain man, she can show that she still respects him by the way that she refuses his offer for a date. Of course, some women are wondering how they can get a date, not turn one down! Nevertheless, let's look at a helpful way to refuse a date.

I've had women turn me down for a date in such a way that I vowed to God I would never ask them for anything again, not even for the time of day. A woman can devastate a man by the way she turns him down. That's one major reason why some men don't ask for a date.

Women may think this is just that old male ego getting stepped on and believe that men put too much stock in it. Some women may even rationalize that it probably does men good to suffer a little rejection. But just remember, women have egos, too. The difference is that the man usually has to take the outward initiative in asking for a date. So when he makes the first move, he has to lay his heart on the line by revealing that he likes her enough to want to go out with her.

In her reply, however, a woman doesn't have to reveal her feelings whatsoever. "I'm so sorry. I have other plans for Friday night" could mean any of the following:

- ▪ "I wish I didn't have other plans so I could go out with you."

- ▪ "Unfortunately, I'm obligated to those plans. Please ask me for another time."

- ▪ "Having other plans gives me some time to think about whether I would want to go out with you."

- ▪ "I'm sure glad I have other plans because I definitely don't want to go out with you!"

- ▪ "I hate to lie about Friday night, but I would say anything to get out of going on a date with you!"

Do you still wonder why a man often becomes timid when asking for a date?

When I was single, there were many, many weekends when I didn't have a date, but not because I had tried and couldn't get one. I was sensitive to the possibility of getting my feelings hurt by a negative reply. I didn't have the emotional strength to hear, "No, I don't want to go out with you."

So how can a woman handle a request for a date? If you don't want to go out, I think it's quite all right to say, the first time, that you're busy that night. You don't have to tell what your plans are, and the man shouldn't ask. It's none of his business that you just may plan to watch television or have a headache that night.

A woman wants a man to initiate a dating relationship, but she wants the right man to do so. The problem is, the man doesn't know if he is the right one. Sometimes a woman is just as unsure. We men have heard stories about other men who kept asking, asking, and asking a woman for months before she would finally go out. Then they ended up getting married. Persistence in those cases paid off. Generally, if a man is asking you out a lot and you don't want to date him, you should be open, honest, and straightforward. By the third invitation, kindly say, "I appreciate your asking me, but I don't want to go out with you."

You may have a difficult time being so blunt, particularly since a woman would rather a man pick up on her subtle hints that she isn't interested. But a man's mind isn't tuned in to picking up subtle hints. He needs to hear it straight. He will at least sense that you respect him if you tell him honestly and compassionately.

A woman should remember that a man wants to hear it straight. When I speak to an all-male audience, I lay my message on the line. The straighter and more accurate I am in getting to the point with a group of men, the better they love it. Of course, tactfulness and caring are greatly appreciated. Don't assume your hints for him to get lost are getting through. He's probably oblivious to them. Honestly and sensitively tell him your feelings and trust God to work in his life.

Some of the greatest lessons of my life came from women breaking up with me. God used the pain to get my attention and teach me what I needed to learn. I am a wiser man for those experiences.

The Band-Aid illustration shows the difference. When I was a little boy, I would try to take a Band-Aid off a cut on my arm. Now, there were two ways to take it off. One was my way. The other was my mother's way. My way was to pull it off slowly, hair by hair, so that it wouldn't hurt. Of course, it still hurt for the half-hour it took to get it off that way. My mother would come over, see me trying to take off the Band-Aid, and say, "Oh, you want to take it off? Here, I'll help you." In a millisecond, she had ripped it off while I was left howling at the top of my lungs. Either way hurt, but at least with my mother's quick and easy method, I got over the pain faster.

The point is that a man and woman can end the uncertainty about going out if the woman will simply tell her thoughts and feelings straight out and get it over with. Then, if he keeps asking her, she has the freedom to say, "I've already told you. I would like to be your friend, but I don't want to have a dating relationship."

Your answer may sting a little, but he will appreciate your openness and show of respect for him. If you try to tell him only through subtle hints, he is likely to take a very long time to get the message. When he does, he probably will blame you for stringing him along for so long, even though your intention was just the opposite.

Love and Good Deeds

For those who have begun a dating relationship, Hebrews 10:23-25 tells us that we are to stimulate one another to love and good deeds. In the social area, we need to pray fervently that the Lord will give us wisdom to mutually respect each other and encourage each other to maximize our lives. For a man, this means doing the small things for a woman like holding a door for her or bringing her flowers to let her know he's been thinking about her. For a woman, it means helping a man think through a problem that he is facing and giving him encouragement.

Of course, sometimes you can get your signals mixed. While I was in Illinois on a speaking tour, I had a couple of dates with a woman who wanted to do everything for herself. She promptly let me know she would rather open her own doors and seat herself in restaurants. Shortly thereafter, I went home to Texas where I had several dates with a woman I had known awhile. At the end of the fourth date, she told me, "I want to talk with you."

"Oh, what about?" I replied.

"You never open a door for me. You never pull out my chair. You never help me out of the car! You are not a gentleman."

I was shell-shocked! What different expectations these two women had. What's the lesson? Be yourself. Be flexible. Treat each other with kindness and respect. Discuss your expecttions and preferences. Above all, trust God for wisdom.

Special Thoughts About Dating

Dating is much more than looking for a potential spouse or having a good time. It is a beautiful opportunity to influence someone else's life and have yours influenced, too. Make it a godly, positive experience. Cultivate healthy attitudes that will enhance a friendship and give depth to your caring. The following are some interesting thoughts you might remember in this regard.

1. Enjoy a Variety of People Before Settling on One

People are fascinating. The range of types of personalities, interests, concerns, and behavior is almost infinite. Get to know lots of different people rather than focusing on one type. The broader your exposure to different people, the clearer your picture of the kind of person you would like to settle down with.

Follow the example of my friend Sean, who wasn't interested in getting serious with anyone. He decided to be friends with lots of women just to be social and to have something to do on weekends. He didn't act too seriously toward any one woman but was friendly and interested in each one. Although Sean was average in looks, his friendliness attracted many women to him. I was curious as why these women wanted to date him.

From Sean, I found out not to worry about what people may think of you. Down-to-earth friendliness and kindness are wonderful virtues. A negative reputation comes from making promises you don't keep or from being a superficial flirt.

If you date more than one person simultaneously, treat each one honestly and respectfully. Avoid being deceitful and coy. Above everything, don't get involved romantically with any of them. If you do, you are actually giving signals to each person that you are committing yourself. If you do that with a couple of people, you will get into trouble—big time. Sooner or later, news of your secretive activities will come to the surface. Being open and honest is the best way to go.

When you find someone who interests you, show that person special attention. Stop dating the others and focus on getting to know the one you like. Don't keep playing the field, especially in your mind. You may be attracted to many, but commit yourself to truly love only one.

Discipline your mind to focus exclusively on the person you are dating. A disciplined mind is one of the greatest gifts you can give to someone in a serious dating relationship. Trouble comes when you grow in your commitment with one person while, at the same time, you keep others around for "social security." Don't develop a fickle heart. "Let love be without hypocrisy."[3]

2. Fun Is Having a Good Time Without Negative Consequences

"We had a great time!" That's what we want to be able to say about a date. Fun, excitement, laughs, satisfaction. The real test of a date, however, is not the response to the activities of one night or one day. It's the attitude and mental, emotional, and spiritual health that are produced through being together over a period of time.

The Bible is the Christian's guidebook for behavior. It gives principles of interacting with people and circumstances that will lead us to personal and relational health. For instance, the Bible says, "Abhor what is evil; cling to what is good."[4]

Keep your heart and conscience under the control of the Holy Spirit. Let the Scriptures saturate your mind and your dating activities. If the person you date asks you to do questionable things, be strong and say no. When "fun" results in negative consequences and guilt, those activities are not worth doing. It's much easier to say no to a person than to face the displeasure of God.

Being with someone who encourages you in your walk with God is always fun. With God at the center of your relationship and activities, you are free to love and to be loved with a love greater than your own, the love that includes His strength and guidance.

3. Be a Builder, Not a Demolitions Expert

As you get to know the person more closely, you will begin to see flaws that you didn't notice in the beginning. In fact, you may not be able to comprehend why anyone would do what your date just did! Some of his or her actions may not only upset you—they may infuriate you. Little annoyances can become major land mines.

What do you do in such a case? Too many people air their frustrations in public with belittling and sarcastic remarks. One couple I know claimed to love one another, but by the way they talked about each other to their friends, I had my doubts. At parties and in other groups, they would gripe about their differences, laughing sarcastically at each other's idiosyncrasies.

One night Paula and I double-dated with them. During that evening they expressed their sorrow about how they had spread negative things about one another. They decided instead to build each other up and to show respect. I applauded their mature decision.

Dating is building the foundation of a long-term relationship. You may not end up marrying each other, but you are developing either a long-term friend or potential adversary. Some of us hold grudges for years after a person has put us down.

Build good memories each time you get together. Then, in the future, you can look back on them with a smile. The apostle Paul said, "Be devoted to one another in brotherly love; give preference to one another in honor; not lagging behind in diligence, fervent in spirit, serving the Lord."[5]

4. Your Public Behavior Reflects the Quality of Your Private Life

People are considered phonies when what they say doesn't match their personal actions. I grew up hearing my father say, "What you do speaks louder than what you say. Talk is cheap."

Notice the consistency between intimate conversations and public behavior. Is the other person (or are you) faithful to personal promises? Beware of (and don't become) the individual who says "You're my honey" in private but acts like "You're a mildewed fig" in public.

Integrity in your private life will show in your public life. We are told that we should be...

> Rejoicing in hope,
>
> persevering in tribulation,
>
> devoted to prayer,
>
> contributing to the needs of the saints [all Christians],
>
> practicing hospitality.[6]

The first three of these are private activities. Hope is founded on God's Word. Cling to Him in troubles and disappointments. Devote yourself to prayer and talking with God.

If you do, your life will exhibit the last two activities, which are practiced in public. Out of a full heart, dedicated to God, you will help others in need. You will be generous and hospitable, opening your home and yourself to entertain and provide for others. You will treat others as you would like to be treated.

Do you and the person you date do these things? A couple should be kind and giving to others. Why don't the two of you throw a party for friends and invite new people from outside your clique to come? Make them feel at home and welcome.

5. An Honest, Spontaneous Compliment Is a Bouquet of Thrills

Have you ever tried to manipulate a compliment out of people? You want them to notice your new car, your latest achievement, or something good you've just done.

When they don't say anything, you're hurt. So you drop hints, hoping they will react with a favorable and vocal response. When they finally do, you're grateful. But it doesn't satisfy as much as if they had noticed spontaneously.

On the other hand, when someone gives you a completely unexpected compliment, you are thrilled. What a surprise! For the rest of the day you think about it.

Learn to notice the details. Be honestly enthusiastic about what pleases you, but without being overbearing and gushy. Too much of a good thing seems forced. Become a saltshaker of compliments, giving just enough to flavor your relationship. When you think something is nice, say so.

Also, learn to take a compliment. It always irked me when a woman would respond to my compliment with a negative statement.

"I like your hair."

"Oh, this greasy mess?"

"That's a pretty dress."

"Really? It's so old."

"Your dinner was delicious."

"Well, it didn't come out as well as I had planned, but I'm glad it was edible."

"You sing so well."

"Oh, I need to practice a lot more than I do."

When someone compliments you, simply say, "Thank you." Then say no more. When you tag your thanks with some remark that belittles the object of the compliment, you belittle the other person's taste or opinion. Many people do this in a false attempt to show personal humility rather than personal pride, but the effort backfires. The person giving the compliment ends up feeling humiliated. Just show gratefulness for kind words and leave it at that.

"Let your speech always be with grace, as though seasoned with salt, so that you will know how you should respond to each person."[7]

6. Friends Are the Window to a Person's Character

If you want to know what is important in the life of the person you are dating, study that person's close friends. As the old saying goes, "Birds of a feather flock together." Friends often reflect a person's values, personality, habits, attitudes, and opinions. Obviously, the friends will differ from the one you are dating in certain areas and even disagree completely on some things. But the reason they are close friends is that they share similar ideas and interests.

Do you enjoy the other person's friends? Can you get along together? If not, once married, when you both relax and stop putting your best foot forward, you may have the same problems in getting along with your new spouse as you did with his or her friends before marriage.

If the person doesn't have friends, he or she may have a difficult time developing close relationships or may prefer to be a loner. If so, you must consider whether this is the type of person you want to marry.

Parents usually know their child better than anyone. They are an important window to a person's true character. How do they feel about their son or daughter dating you? How does the person you are dating treat their parents? Are there tensions, arguments, and misunderstandings? The way a person treats their parents and relatives is a good indicator of how they may eventually treat you. Old habits are difficult to break.

You may want to excuse the person you care about if their parents are divorced or just plain disagreeable. But, if this is so, he or she may not have learned from them how to relate well with other people while growing up. Learning from Dad and Mom how to relate to a spouse is intended to be part of the growing-up process.

The person you like may not have learned from his or her parents how to develop an intimate marriage. He or she may have observed what not to do. Has your potential spouse since learned and put into practice positive ways to relate successfully with other people? If not, when in a tough situation in your relationship, he or she is likely to revert to attitudes and behaviors his or her parents demonstrated.

7. Keep the Child in You Alive

Children are curious about everything. Their minds delve into all kinds of areas that are mysteries to them. They are not afraid to ask questions and seek answers. Their world is filled with fun and new discoveries.

If you lose the childlike desire to find something new and exciting in ordinary things, you will become dull and boring. Too many singles become so serious about daily existence and its problems that they forget to be thrilled and excited about the ordinary things of life.

Become an interesting person by developing an interest in life and in other people. On a date or while talking on the phone, ask thought-provoking questions and listen intently to answers. Together, enjoy the simple things in life— walking in the park, reading a book, playing tennis, going window-shopping, looking at the stars. Develop a sense of curiosity and enjoyment about God's world and life itself.

One of the best dates I ever had could have been a disaster. I had planned to take Lynne to a nice restaurant and then to a movie. After paying for the meal, I counted my remaining cash and realized all I had left was $5.76. What do I do now? I had forgotten to go to the ATM that day. I didn't have my checkbook or credit card. I was embarrassed at my predicament.

Finally I thought of an idea. I said, "Lynne, tonight you have a great opportunity. We are going to do something that may surprise you, a change of plans." I showed her my money. "I'm going to give you all my money, with two stipulations. First, you have to spend all of it tonight—every penny. Second, you have to take me along."

I then proceeded, laboriously, to pull out five one-dollar bills and seventy-six cents in change, a coin at a time. The dismayed look on her face made me feel uneasy, but I kept going with my idea. "Let's think of the good points of this situation. I didn't realize how little money I had with me tonight, but we can still have a great time, if we try, with $5.76."

So we sat there, trying to decide what to do. It was tough at first. Do you know how many things you can buy for $5.76? Very few.

As we started to go around town with our money, we went into a number of stores that didn't seem to have anything interesting for $5.76. Finally, we ended up in a cheap discount store, looking at balloons. You can buy a lot of balloons for $5.76. But as we thought about sitting around that night trying to blow them up, we decided against the idea. Finally, we settled on a 500-piece jigsaw puzzle that was marked down to $4.99 and a crumpled candy bar on a table of closeouts for $.39. Believe it or not, with tax, they added up to exactly $5.76. Making our purchases took two hours.

We then went to Lynne's apartment, laughing about our unique treasure hunt. We occasionally ate tiny bits of the mashed candy bar so that it would last the rest of the evening, and we worked on the puzzle. It was a great time—a date I'll always remember. Learn to be creative and enjoy the simple things.

Two Roads

Relating together socially is part of learning how to mold two distinct lives toward a common unit. Two roads begin to merge into one through all their twists and turns. Yet differences will always remain. That can be intriguing—as well as irritating.

You may have decided that the differences in interests and behavior prohibit a serious relationship. A mature couple allows this realization to be the crossroad where each one goes a separate way, but both feel they are richer and wiser for the experience of their time together.

But if you decide you enjoy each other's company enough to work out the differences, then social intimacy can be a rich experience that builds toward a beautiful friendship or even a successful marriage.

5

Your Mental Life: Discovering How You Think

SOCIAL

The
MENTAL

No matter how much we appreciate people, we have to realize that even those we love and respect most are going to differ with the way we think in certain areas. All relationships include big differences. Every couple will have arguments and heated discussions.

During our many months of dating and engagement, Paula and I never had a major disagreement. After we got married, we had our first big clash. It happened on our first trip together to shop in a grocery store. Paula hates to go grocery shopping, so she always maps out a plan of action, her P.O.A. She thinks through exactly what items she wants to get beforehand and makes a list. When she goes into the store, she looks only for the exact items on that list. She wants to get out of the store as soon as possible.

Not me! I go to the grocery store for a vacation. I look forward to seeing the latest displays and all the new products. I'm away from my desk, and I leave the cell phone in the car. No one can reach me. I love to walk up and down each aisle, slowly observing everything that's there. I can spend hours in a grocery store.

When we entered the store, I slowly sauntered down the aisles, curiously looking at everything. Paula was determined to get out of there as soon as possible. She rushed from one section to another, grabbing only what she had already decided to buy. She said several times, "Dick, come on, hurry up!" And I responded, "Honey, slow down. Let's enjoy ourselves. Do you know they have over 50 different kinds of cereal? I can't decide which ones we should get. Let's try something new."

She was rushing to get out of there, and I was trying to slow her down so we could enjoy the experience. Right there in Aisle 7, we had a big argument. It was the first time in 42 years that I had a difficult time in a grocery store. After many discussions and adjustments, we learned that when we shop together, we have to have a mutual P.O.A. Paula says, "Dick, you get the bread and the yogurt." That's the only responsibility I have. She gets 20 items, and I get 2. By the time she gets her 20 items, I'm still looking at the bread—trying to find that perfect loaf that is tasty, inexpensive, and healthy. I may take a long time to choose, but I leave the grocery store satisfied that I've made the best purchases of bread and yogurt for us. Meanwhile, Paula got her 20 items in record time.

We could have solved the problem differently. We could have agreed never to go to the grocery store together. But that might have carried over to not going many other places together. I could have insisted that she learn to saunter slowly along with me, while she got more and more anxious about spending so much time aimlessly. Or, to keep peace, I might have rushed through the store with her, becoming frustrated that I had no opportunity to check out new items or to experience the sense of rejuvenation I get from losing myself in a grocery store.

Uniqueness and Oneness

Those inadequate solutions would have violated what, I believe, are the two major goals in relating with someone of the opposite sex. The first goal is to respect that person's uniqueness. He or she is a unique creation of God whose thinking and feeling differs with yours. As you develop your relationship, learn to understand the other person as much as possible. Don't try to force him or her to become like you—how boring!

The second goal in establishing a relationship is to build oneness, preserving each person's uniqueness while developing unity. Oneness doesn't mean becoming exactly like each other. It's never good to force another person to be like you. Someone has said, "If two are the same, one is not needed." Consider the apostles Peter and Paul. They differed with each other, but they had oneness of mind in serving the Lord.

In writing about marital oneness between a husband and wife, the apostle Peter said, "To sum up, let all be harmonious, sympathetic, brotherly, kindhearted, and humble in spirit; not returning evil for evil or insult for insult, but giving a blessing instead; for you were called for the very purpose that you might inherit a blessing."[1] This doesn't mean that two people in a relationship should think exactly the same. You'll never find two people who do that.

"Let all be harmonious" means that you learn to build oneness together. To be like-minded is to have the same goals and purposes as you grow together. God has given each of us different gifts. Sometimes some of the gifts don't seem to mesh. In a dating relationship, one person may be outgoing, bubbly, active, hopping quickly from one exciting idea and plan to another. The other person may be slow about things and want to think more deeply before making any move at all. This is usually the one who sees all the little details and presents all the reasons why an idea won't work. He or she tends to pour cold water on the onslaught of ideas that the effervescent person is certain can be carried out.

Cautious thinkers often ask, "But will it really work?" and interject realism into the situation. On the other hand, idealistic, high-energy people head toward their exciting goals in overdrive, outdistancing other people. But in their haste to reach the desired destination, they may either strip the gears or crash into obstacles they never considered. At the same time, detail people may have a difficult time just getting into first gear. They need the bright ideas of another person to get them going. These God-given traits that seem to clash were given to us for a purpose—to help us balance one another.

God wants us to learn to work together in a coordinated manner. This applies to all relationships in life. By appreciating the God-given character traits of people who differ with us, we can work together to accomplish God's purposes.

Instead of saying, "You've got to be like me," Paula and I have learned to preserve each other's uniqueness while working on becoming one, not only on shopping trips but in other areas of our lives as well.

The Joy of Discovery

Across America, one of the questions I hear often is, Why don't men communicate more? I don't think the problem is that men can't talk. I think men have difficulty talking about their own lives, feelings, and opinions. They can talk for hours with a colleague about their work or with a fellow enthusiast about a favorite sport or hobby. Other than that, men often communicate only in short sentences.

Women, on the other hand, love details. Have you ever noticed the difference between a man and a woman when answering a simple question? You ask a man, "Was Joe at the party last night?" "Yeah" is the most frequent reply you'll get.

Ask a woman the same question and she is likely to reply, "Sure, Joe was there. He seemed really happy now that he has changed jobs. I liked what he was wearing, especially his shirt. You know, I think he looks awkward on the dance floor. Someone needs to give him some dance lessons."

Most women are interested in details, feelings, and opinions. They assume other people are, too. Most men need to learn to be more detail-oriented. Talk details and a woman will love it.

Men, on the other hand, enjoy activities. They often communicate through actions. A woman can learn a lot about a man by getting involved in a sport, hobby, or social event with him.

To be of the same mind as someone else, which is an important part of developing intimacy, you must discover how another person thinks and allow the other person to learn how you think. Developing the mental area of our Relationship Star can be a fascinating journey. Let's consider some ideas on how to discover what is in someone else's mind.

1. Discover How the Other Person Makes Decisions

Is he or she logical in approaching life? Does this person get all the facts together and then make a decision? Or does he or she make a decision quickly and then change that decision several times? Does this person contemplate a situation a long time before making a decision and then, having made it, refuse to reconsider? Or does he or she decide and then continually worry if it is right, struggling to carry out the decision? Learning the decision-making process that other people use helps us understand them.

2. Learn How to Listen

Do you usually talk but rarely listen? For instance, have you ever had a conversation with another person that was actually two monologues going on at the same time? You say something. That reminds the other person of a different subject, so she interrupts you with her own statement. You pay no attention to what is now being said because you're only waiting to get back to what you were saying in the first place. This is not a meeting of the minds. Two people are talking, but no one is listening. Constantly interrupting other people shows you don't respect them and are only interested in talking about your own interests.

Some people must have an opportunity to complete their communication before they can switch mental gears and listen to others. Learn how other people listen. Gear your conversations according to the way they listen.

3. Learn How to Ask Open-Ended Questions

I have been amazed at the number of people who don't know how to question others. They talk but don't listen very well. Good communication is a two-way street—expressing and listening.

Whenever another person makes a statement, don't let that be the end of the communication. Ask open-ended questions about a subject. These are questions that can't be answered with a yes or a no.

If you ask, "Did you have a good day?" the answer will be yes or no. After that, the conversation dies. Giving a short reply without divulging any significant information is too easy.

But if you ask, "How was your day?" the answer can't be yes or no. An explanation is expected. When seeking to understand, use the five Ws and H—who, what, when, where, why, and how. "Who is your closest friend at work?" "What was the most important thing you did this week?" "Why do you like (or dislike) your work?" "When do you hope to finish that big project you're working on?" "How are you handling the pressures you are facing?" If you use these key words, people will have to talk more and reveal their inner feelings, values, and perspectives.

4. Discover the Reasons Behind a Person's Opinions

Ask questions that reveal other people's opinions and how those opinions were formed. Why do they think the way they do on such subjects as politics, sports, and current social issues? As time goes on, especially in marriage, knowing why another person thinks in a particular way becomes more and more important.

5. Expand Your Minds

Communication can be interesting. Don't be fooled into thinking it's a dull way to pass the time. To add variety to your conversations, read books and other literature that will help you learn to talk intelligently on subjects besides the weather and sports. Read a weekly news magazine and discuss something in it that interests you or the other person. Learn to discuss issues in life that are affecting people and nations.

If you marry, you will spend thousands of hours alone with your spouse. You had better *want* to spend thousands of hours alone! If your time alone now is primarily a make-out scene, you will have a hard time in marriage finding something to do together for a lifetime. Long evenings, five nights a week, and the 48 hours that make up Saturday and Sunday, year in and year out, require us to find something more than physical attraction to enjoy each other's company for 40 or 50 years.

Of course, at first we are all attracted to another person's outward appearance. But as someone joked, "Time may be a healer of wounds, but it is a lousy beautician." As we get older, our bodies deteriorate. What looked very attractive at age 20 may look unattractive at 60. However, though the body inevitably wilts, the mind and character of a person can keep on growing and blossoming. As you seek a spouse, give more attention to the inner life and mind.

Instead of communicating like TV newscasters announcing the latest facts on the evening news program without emotion or opinion, ask open-ended questions seeking to learn more about a person's thoughts and opinions. Listen intently and seek to understand why a person feels and thinks the way they do.

Sharing Common Interests

I like antiques, especially antique American oak furniture and advertising signs. Teaching other people about them brings me lots of joy. I think one of the greatest ways to have fun with someone else is to go to an antique auction. It doesn't cost a thing, unless you raise your hand. Just watching the auctioneer is an experience in itself. Playing a guessing game about the sale price for an item is an education in the value people place on old things. Learning why one item goes for $5 and another for $500 can be fascinating.

For years, I looked forward to the prospect of antiquing with my future spouse. What a blow it was to find out that Paula knew nothing about antiques! They were simply old things to her. However, when she realized how much I enjoyed looking at antiques and going to auctions, she decided to learn to appreciate them more for my sake. On the other hand, Paula loves to take long walks early in the morning. Not me—I like to play racquetball and jog. But when I discovered her preference for walks, I became interested in walking with her. We have found activities and interests that we now enjoy doing together. Why? Because they bring us together.

You probably have a favorite interest or activity that you can share with another person. In fact, try to have many so that you can enjoy those things together. Even though opposites attract, the more common interests you have, the broader the foundation you will have to build a relationship that will be fulfilling.

Differences Call for Commitment

An important part of the mental area of relationships is the way we handle differences. Working out differences is a major problem in our fast-paced, changeable world. Today, many people go by the rally cry, "Get in there and quit!" Sometimes I think our society is made up of lots of people who, if they don't like something or find it difficult, just drop it and go on to other things.

Commitment has become a foreign word. When is the last time you heard anyone say they were committed to something for a lifetime?

Because committing to one person in marriage for a lifetime is not considered important, divorce is an option millions of couples choose. A major reason for this is that few people learn to work out their differences while remaining committed to the relationship to make it succeed. Maintaining your marriage through thick and thin isn't easy if you haven't already learned how to work through differences in other relationships.

Handling Differences the Wrong Way

What happens when you cannot agree on something? What are some negative ways to resolve your differences?

One way is to withdraw from the conflict by giving the silent treatment or sulking. If you have a difference or hurt feelings, you just stop communicating with the other person. You don't call, or you refuse to talk about the problem the next time you are together. You walk by the other person as if he or she doesn't exist.

Although this kind of reaction is all too common, I do not recommend it as a way of dealing with conflicts. In a relationship, silence is not golden—it's just yellow. In fact, it's downright cowardly to avoid the subject (or a growing list of subjects) on which you disagree. If you want to build oneness, you both need to talk about your feelings and differences. I've known couples who have gone weeks without discussing why they have stopped talking about certain subjects with each other. This avoidance will lead to isolation.

Some people handle differences by holding a grudge. They indulge in the "I'll forgive you but I'll never forget" attitude. They store up the grudges like ammunition in a closet. At the appropriate moment in a discussion, they bring out all the unresolved conflicts and blast away.

The Bible says that God not only forgives but also forgets our sins. David writes in the Psalms, "As far as the east is from the west, so far has He removed our transgressions from us."[2] And the prophet Micah tells us that God will "hurl all our iniquities into the depths of the sea."[3] They will be buried so deeply that they will never be found again. The prayer that the Lord taught us includes asking God to "forgive us our debts [trespasses, sins], as we also have forgiven our debtors."[4] We need to forgive, heal wounds, and consciously decide to let go of any vengeful attitudes. We do this for our own sake as well as for the sake of building oneness in our relationships.

Accept Yourself

An important part of learning to accept another person is learning to accept yourself first. If you don't accept yourself, you are likely to try to mold the other person into some ideal image that you have concocted. Unsure of yourself, you will try to convince yourself and others that your way of doing things is the only correct way. Or you're likely to want the other person to have characteristics that you think you lack and need. In that way, you might have better status with others as a couple than you think you do as an individual.

The ability to develop a satisfying intimate relationship depends, first of all, on accepting yourself as a recipient of God's love and grace. Christ died on the cross for you. And He now receives you just as you are when you come to Him. What greater proof of your worthiness can there be?

"For by grace you have been saved through faith; and that not of yourselves, it is the gift of God; not as a result of works, that no one may boast."[5] Because He accepts you where you are in life, you can accept others the way they are. Why try to force change in another person to fit your ideal picture of what they should look like?

Don't misunderstand. God does expect us to improve and mature. If, after failing, we repent, He always accepts us where we are and gives us another chance. His Holy Spirit motivates and empowers us to do better the next time with the unique abilities He has given each of us. In the same way, we can give other people the same type of freedom and encouragement.

Steps Toward Mental Intimacy

Paula and I have learned that to handle differences positively, we must first of all *recognize that we do have differences.* And it's okay to be different. If you seem to have no differences with another person, something is wrong. No two people in the world are exactly alike. One of you may not be showing your true feelings about matters, perhaps for fear of offending or losing the other person.

Second, *appreciate the other person's opinions and ways of doing things*. The other person comes from a different background, has a different personality, and has different learned ways of doing things. God has made each of you unique with strengths and weaknesses, spiritual gifts, parental upbringing, and life experiences. Enjoy the process of discovering the complexity and variety in each other's life.

Third, endeavor to *put yourself in the other person's shoes*. Try to understand that person's perspective. For some of us, this is very hard to do. We are either so talkative, so argumentative, so stubborn, or so intent on getting the other person to agree with our perspective that we never stop to think where the other person is coming from.

Fourth, *express yourself honestly*. Don't cover up your feelings with a smile, saying everything is okay when it isn't. Talk about things honestly and lovingly.

Fifth, *take steps to improve your communication and develop oneness*. You may not be able or willing to resolve some issues. Face the possibility that the Lord may want you to break off your dating relationship. If, however, you think you can learn to accept each other's differences and appreciate each other's ways, you will draw closer together.

Learning to come to a meeting of the minds—building oneness while respecting and appreciating each other's uniqueness—is a major step on the road to forming a balanced Relationship Star.

6

Your Emotional Life: Understanding Your Feelings

■ ■ ■

SOCIAL

MENTAL

The EMOTIONAL

Joseph was engaged to a really great woman and was looking forward to their marriage. One day she said, "Joseph, you're not going to believe this."

"What, Mary?"

"Ummm, well...Joseph, I'm pregnant."

"You're pregnant! Who is the guy? Where is he?"

"No, no, Joseph. You don't understand. It's God."

"God? Look, Mary, I know the facts of life. It doesn't happen like that. A woman gets pregnant when she has sex with a man."

"I know, Joseph...but it's God."

"Oh, really? Well, how do you know?"

"An angel told me."

"An angel told you that it was God? Humph!"

This illustrated segment of the events surrounding the birth of Jesus puts a lot more human drama and emotion into the Christmas story than what most of us picture when we hear the following recited at Christmastime:

> Now the birth of Jesus Christ was as follows: when His mother Mary had been betrothed to Joseph, before they came together she was found to be with child by the Holy Spirit. And Joseph her husband, being a righteous man, and not wanting to disgrace her, planned to send her away [divorce her] secretly.
>
> But when he had considered this, behold, an angel of the Lord appeared to him in a dream, saying, "Joseph, son of David, do not be afraid to take Mary as your wife; for that which has been conceived in her is of the Holy Spirit. And she will bear a Son; and you shall call His name Jesus, for He will save His people from their sins."
>
> Now all this took place to fulfill what was spoken by the Lord through the prophet: "Behold, the virgin shall be with child and shall bear a Son, and they shall call His name Immanuel," which translated means, "God with us."
>
> And Joseph awoke from his sleep and did as the angel of the Lord commanded him, and took Mary as his wife, but kept her a virgin until she gave birth to a Son; and he called His name Jesus.[1]

Can't you imagine Joseph tossing and turning all night after he first learned that Mary was pregnant? The drama that must have been going on inside him isn't too hard to comprehend. If anyone ever wanted to believe in a virgin birth, surely Joseph did, even though it was contrary to all known facts. But did you ever consider what Joseph's emotions must have been when he heard the news that his fiancée, with whom he had never had sexual relations, was pregnant?

Someone said to me a long time ago, "Remember, Dick, behind every face there's a drama going on. Tap into the drama." In relationships, we need to discover the drama going on inside other people's lives. What is so interesting about human life is that the drama doesn't stop. It's a never-ending saga. The more you tap into the drama, the more exciting your life becomes.

Even in our church groups and Bible studies, I believe we should discuss more than just the facts about Joseph and other biblical figures. We should look under the surface of biblical events to find the characters' emotions. We can then tap into the real drama of these events, learn how biblical characters dealt with their feelings, and, from that, learn more about how to lead our own lives in a godly manner.

Sharing Feelings Is Important

You can apply this to life around you as well. When you see someone act or react, don't just look at the surface situation. Try to discover what's going on underneath the surface. Ask questions such as, "What makes you feel angry…loved …accepted…rejected?"

Neglecting the opportunity to understand the emotional makeup of another person is all too easy. Not only is it a time-consuming task, but the other person's feelings can easily affect yours, and emotions are hard to control. As a result, many friendships develop a lopsided Relationship Star.

Today's society gives poor advice in this area: Play it cool. Show him or her who is boss. Play hard to get. Don't show your emotions. Keep them guessing. Be in control.

I disagree with this thinking completely. I strongly believe that we should expose our emotions in a relationship, not cover them up. We need to know each other's inner feelings if we are to achieve a balanced Relationship Star and intimate friendship, even though there are no easy ways to go about this.

Have you noticed that just the way you look at a person may make them feel rejected? Once I was eating in a romantic, candlelit restaurant with my girlfriend Britney, who suddenly asked me, "Is there anything wrong?"

"Wrong?" I responded, "Nothing's wrong. Why do you ask?"

"Well, you just look like something is wrong."

"No, there's nothing wrong."

"Are you sure? You looked at me as if something were wrong."

"Well, I've got a lot on my mind."

What makes a person like Britney sense problems? What makes a person feel lonely? What makes a person feel secure or insecure? Discuss questions like these with people who mean a lot to you. Ask these same questions of yourself.

Differences in Communication Styles

Many difficulties in a relationship stem from the different ways men and women tend to communicate. As children, boys and girls learn to communicate very differently.

Girls learn a lot about interpersonal communication from playing with dolls when they are young. A little girl has a cute baby doll, a hunk of plastic and fuzz, to which she gives a name. She either gently combs its hair or throws it across the room, depending on her mood. A little girl talks to her doll and may even play school in order to teach it something. She also has a doll house with all kinds of imaginary people living in it. She learns to relate her thoughts and feelings by communicating with her dolls. And how do little boys learn to communicate? Their main interests are toy soldiers, guns, and trucks. "Vroom, vroom, vroom." His vocabulary usually starts out with one syllable sounds and words that express his interaction with the world around him.

"Bang, bang, you're dead," he says to a friend who is playing with him.

"I am not."

"Yes, you are."

"No, I'm not!"

In this way, little boys learn to communicate. Along with relating to objects, boys learn to stifle their emotions. Mom and Dad and other people warn, "Big boys don't cry." And as boys grow up, others teach them to refrain from sharing their feelings. "When you get knocked down in football, don't lay on the ground crying." Think of some of the images portrayed by movies. The tough commando speeds into town with his machine gun mowing down the terrorists and blowing up enemy fortifications. In a few minutes he wipes out all the bad guys and then struts confidently away. He doesn't say much. He doesn't have to. His guns and explosives have done the talking for him. Can you imagine him telling a woman, "I have a personal problem. Can you help me?"

Television also brings us a constant barrage of football, hockey, and other contact sports in which huge, muscular hulks smash violently into their opponents. But do you ever see the players shed a tear? Never. Finally, the debilitated gladiator gets up and hobbles to the sidelines.

And the crowd cheers and yells for the courageous felled player. Then, as the crowd's attention returns to the game, the player collapses on the sidelines. But not when people's attention is on him! He stuffs his emotions and pain away, never allowing others to see his agony. All our lives men learn to hide their emotions in front of other people and move on.

When a man develops a close relationship with a woman, he finds out that she's not like his sports coach who yelled, "Suck up your gut and get back in the game!" She wants him to express his emotions. "A woman wants to know my feelings? The deep-inside me?" Some of us men have hidden behind a hardened exterior, behind the successes we've strived for, for so long that we're not sure we can pull out our feelings to show them. After all, if ever we've shared our hearts with other guys in school or on the team, they've usually joked about it. We don't like to be mocked, so we have stifled our feelings and emotions most of our lives.

Then a woman we care about starts asking very difficult questions. Why are you upset? How do you feel about that? What do you want to do with your life? She wants to know a man's heart. Why? Because she wants to be part of his life. Because she cares for him. Her desire is to help him grow and develop.

Some men try to communicate their inner being and feelings. But they have stifled everything for so long that they have shriveled up inside. Deep within they know they have a sensitive heart. But they rarely see models of men displaying such sensitivity, so they don't know how to do it. One man said to me after one of my conferences on relationships, "Okay, I'll share my emotions with my girlfriend. But what are they?"

Men Need to Express Emotions

I suggest that a man take the emotional risk to begin to share what's deep down in his soul. He might be amazed how others, particularly his girlfriend, will respond.

During one period in my life, I struggled with trying to decide what to do with my life and career. I was an assistant pastor in a church, but I didn't know what to do about my future. I knew that I didn't want to continue in that position. I wanted to be a senior pastor, but I was 36 and single. No church wanted a single senior pastor. I had three or four other options, but everything seemed to be failing and falling apart. I didn't know what to do about my future.

While my girlfriend and I were sitting in her apartment, she asked me, "Dick, what are you going to do in the future?" I started to give her a controlled, superficial reply. But suddenly my confused feelings began to come out, and I felt like I was going to cry. Immediately two alternatives came to my mind. First, if I continued to cry, I figured she would reject me. I could just imagine her telling her friends, "My boyfriend is a real crybaby." But second, if I didn't tell her my heart and stifled everything inside again, I thought I would burst.

I had to tell somebody, and she was the only one around. So I decided, *Okay, I'll open the floodgates and spill my insides. It will probably be the last time she will ever want to see me, but here goes.*

I told her all my fears and shared all my struggles and confusion. For a half hour I let it pour out. When I was finished, I asked her, "What do you think about all I've said?"

I was amazed at her answer. She said, "This makes me love you all the more."

Astonished, I replied, "It does?"

I had expected rejection. What she said, in essence, was that she wanted to share in my struggles, and she saw areas in which she thought she could help me.

Revealing your true emotions in a relationship is very difficult, especially for a man. He needs to learn how to communicate some of those deep inner thoughts and feelings in a relationship with a woman. He does not need to manufacture some problem to talk about, nor does he have to cry when he tells it. But he does need to learn to share what's really important to him.

Women Need to Explain Emotions

A woman, too, may have difficulty communicating emotions. Usually, she doesn't mind expressing her thoughts and feelings. But when a man asks his girlfriend, "What's wrong?" she will say, "Nothing." She assumes he should figure things out. Somehow, putting her emotions into words minimizes them. The problem is, he doesn't know what's going on inside of her. If a woman wants to develop emotional intimacy and understanding with her boyfriend, she needs to put her feelings into words.

So where does she go for advice to try to understand her man? To her woman friends. She will tell them her frustrations and get their counsel for a solution. They will all get together and discuss their opinions. Finally, her friends arrive at a collective decision. So she decides to follow their advice about how to solve the situation.

She goes back to her man to try it and finds out it doesn't always work! Why? Her female friends may have some understanding of men, but it is limited to their feminine perspective. A woman who wants to help solve a problem she is having with a man may receive excellent advice about what to do by going to another man to get his opinion. Try it and see. Men will usually better understand other men than women do. The reverse is also true.

Hurting Others and Being Hurt

Another area of emotions involves the fear of hurting others. Most of us don't want to bring pain into someone else's life. When we are afraid that we will hurt the other person, we keep quiet about subjects that need to be discussed. Deep inside, we may be keeping quiet for fear of getting hurt ourselves.

A person who is afraid of hurting someone usually sees himself or herself in a position of power in the relationship and the other person in a position of weakness.

When we are overly fearful of hurting others, we usually misunderstand how God works in people's lives. Often God uses hurt to teach His children great lessons. The Lord has often used disappointments or broken relationships to teach me some important lessons. He has done that when various women broke off dating relationships with me. Don't try to play the role of the Holy Spirit in people's lives by protecting them from hurt. Allow the Spirit to work in their lives—and in your life.

Sandi had a lot of concerns about her boyfriend's wild past. Tim had sexual relationships with several women before he became a Christian. Sandi's fears that he had not changed his ways kept growing. Although they were engaged, she was afraid to talk to Tim about these fears. She knew that talking about his past would be painful for him, so she just swept her fears under the rug.

In reality, Sandi didn't want to discuss the situation because she might be the one to get hurt. She was afraid of finding out something that would harm this "dream" relationship.

Situations like this are especially devastating. The relationship starts out in a beautiful fantasy realm, and as it grows, romantic feelings race ahead of the rest of the relationship. When doubts and questions come regarding the other person's habits, past, or negative qualities, we hold back from bringing these doubts into the light. After all, who wants to bring reality into Disneyland? It only takes away from the fun.

But no one can live in Disneyland for long. So a boiling cauldron of smothered emotions begins to build up pressure underneath the surface and to shake the foundations of the dreamlike existence. Often, one person or the other senses the uneasiness but finds it difficult to discuss openly. They cover their fears when what they really need to do is expose them and talk about them even though this would be painful.

Losing Control

Another fear is that of losing control. Most of us want to control our own lives, including situations that involve other people. We try to make things work out the way we envision or desire because we want to be happy, and we think we know how to accomplish that. We want to keep the upper hand in controlling a relationship so we don't get hurt.

Dating relationships reveal the insecurities in our lives. We wonder about the future. *Is this the one for me?* We try to avoid rejection at all costs. Because we worry about the other person turning on us or leaving, we hesitate to show our vulnerability and to be open with our questions and doubts.

Tony, for instance, has dated several women. He once told me that he was dating a certain girl, but he was getting scared. "What are you afraid of?" I asked.

"I'm afraid I'm losing control," he replied. "Previously, I've been able to have the upper hand in relationships. But I can no longer control this one. My feelings of love and my desire for commitment and marriage are getting out of hand—beyond my ability to control. I'm afraid I'm getting into an area where I can be hurt by her and hurt deeply."

Men and Vulnerability

Men are often leery of vulnerability. We are afraid to let anyone see our failures and the habits that are not always positive. To expose what we've tried to cover up for many years is very difficult.

For a man, the areas hardest to reveal involve his weaknesses. The areas of a dating relationship that are tender spots include his fears of not being a good lover and of not being able to remain committed to a woman for a lifetime. He fears intimacy because a woman will want to know these feelings and the other issues that affect his life. So he holds back until he feels he's in much better control. He wants to have all of his bases covered before he gets up to the plate.

I had wanted to date Annette for two years. I would see her every July at our organization's two-week training conference, but I would never ask her out. I was too afraid she might not like me. Finally, I worked up enough courage to ask her out during the third July conference.

I called her the first day. "Hi, Annette!" I said. "I just arrived for the conference. Would you like to go out this evening and get something to eat?"

"I'd like to, Dick," she replied, "but I've planned to do something else."

So, the second day, I called her again and asked her out.

"I'd like to," she said, "but I already have some plans."

The third day I tried again. "I'd like to, but...." Eight straight days I asked her out and got the same answer.

I will never forget the ninth day. I called her up and again asked her if she would like to go out. "I would like to," she replied, "but the conference is almost over, and I'm going to be busy for the rest of it. Why don't you ask me next year?"

You know what suddenly hit me? She didn't want to go out with me! I was bothering her! I had been rejected and hadn't even realized it!

I felt so embarrassed because I hadn't picked up on her feelings sooner. You see, I had been hearing the words, "I would like to go out with you." I tuned out the words, "I have other plans." She was implying, "I don't want to go out with you." In this situation, I definitely had made myself vulnerable to hurt. I had not picked up her disinterest in dating me. But in the process I learned that I needed to be more aware and better able to be sensitive to what a woman implies and hints. And Annette definitely needed to learn how to communicate and "tell it like it is."

Women and Change

A woman may be afraid of having to change her career direction for a man. Should she continue with the sense of direction she has already chosen for her life? Or should she consider adapting her choice to a man's career direction?

Believing that God led her to her present career may make the decision even more difficult. Sometimes, she keeps quiet about the dedication she has to her work goals, leaving the impression that fitting into the man's life plan would be no problem. However, when the relationship becomes serious, the issue finally has to be faced.

I talked with Greg, a Christian businessman from Atlanta, and his girlfriend, Janie, as they were taking me to the airport. He told me that for two years he had asked her repeatedly to marry him, but she would not say yes. Janie wanted to go back to school and train to become an overseas missionary. She wanted him to go with her. But he felt his direction and goal in life was to become a prominent businessman and to make lots of money. Their different purposes created a struggle. He didn't want Janie to leave Atlanta to return to school for her desired career.

Finally, Greg submitted to Janie's wishes and she moved away to school. Still, he constantly told her that she should forget her plans to live in another country, become his wife, and live in Atlanta. They struggled and manipulated each other. Both were trying to get the other to go along with their own perspective. Both were afraid to lose the struggle, but both were also afraid to give up. They were caught in the awful middle where their relationship just muddled through. Greg and Janie needed to give their relationship over to the Lord, to let Him work out whatever He wanted for their relationship and for each of them individually.

Obeying God's will for your life is far more important—and ultimately more satisfying—than fulfilling someone else's (or your own) selfish desires. What has God put into your heart? Do that, and let Him take care of the future.

Emotional Intimacy

The emotional area is a sensitive one because you are a sensitive being. You want to be loved and to love, to belong to someone. You have a great urge to knock down the walls of secrecy and to reveal the deep-down-inside you. If you are interested in getting to know the person better, let the deep-down-inside you be seen. Building understanding about each other's feelings and sensitivities is a long, sometimes tortuous road, but it is well worth the effort.

1. Learn to Observe Details

Observe what a person likes or dislikes. Pick up non-verbal signs, such as a frown, a slammed door, a sudden silence, or a swift change of subject. Then, communicating interest and curiosity, ask for the reason behind the action or statement. Observe how a person relates with other people. What causes discouragement? What brings encouragement? Relate on those issues.

Men, you will be amazed how far such thoughtfulness will go for a woman. We men think that when we ask a woman out for a date, all we have to do to make it a fantastic time is spend a lot of money. Sometimes women are more interested in simpler things, such as just talking and relating. Use the key words learned in the last chapters: who, what, when, where, why, and how. Both of you can learn a lot about each other's feelings.

2. Recognize the Need for Space and Timing

We don't like to fail or to lose control. Dating relationships are always risky. You may have a tendency to hold back and let the other person take the initiative. Don't wait for your friend to start the discussion. Talk about your real self and ask questions to stimulate further transparency between the both of you.

If the other person doesn't want to talk about something, however, immediately back off. Give some emotional space. Timing is an important part of building emotional intimacy.

After I finish a presentation at a seminar or convention, I am sensitive to criticism. I've given it my best shot, and I hope the audience has responded favorably. Paula has come to realize that the best time to help me improve my presentations is a few hours after I have finished or the next day. By then I have calmed down and can look at the content and delivery of my speech more objectively. Paula then discusses with me its positive and negative factors and encourages me to become more effective. She has learned when to interact and when it's better to be silent.

3. Build an Emotional Refuge

The world batters us and degrades our humanity. Intimate friendships can provide a refuge from the attacks of society. You should feel free enough with each other to discuss the full range of your feelings, both positive and negative. Don't hide behind an Off-Limits sign. Learn to accept each other for the real people you are.

A word of warning in this regard. One of the worst mistakes you can make after someone has expressed his or her true feelings to you is to tell other friends all the details. Nothing angers a person more than to hear that something told in trust has become common knowledge. A confidence has been betrayed. The hurt will cause the other person to withdraw from you emotionally. Private conversations are private knowledge. Build trust in each other. That encourages further sharing and openness. Scripture says, "Bear one another's burdens, and thereby fulfill the law of Christ."[2]

4. Monitor Your Emotional Intensity

At the beginning of a relationship, don't let strong emotions build too fast. Too many couples get overly excited at the start of their relationship. When they meet someone who makes the heart pound wildly, they spend many hours together, day after day. They can't get enough of each other. This may be "the one"!

Then reality strikes. Each one notices things about the other that are disturbing. They get tired of being together so much. They don't want to acknowledge this for fear the other person will take it in the wrong way and break up.

Don't allow this kind of pressure to destroy a potentially good relationship. You may be indulging in too much talk about "us and the future." If your relationship becomes over-analyzed, the fun will be lost and the relationship will become drudgery.

Back up in your emotional intensity. Give each other some freedom to be alone or to be with other friends. For a while, put a moratorium on serious conversations about where your relationship is headed. Emphasize mutual understanding, honesty, and enjoyment. Allow time for slower, more solid growth. Be yourself, and if the person doesn't like who you are, that person is not the one for you. Part on friendly terms, respecting each other's uniqueness and personality.

5. Balance Your Heart and Your Head

We have a tendency to go too much toward one extreme or the other. You don't want to become either an emotional basket case or an unfeeling machine. You need the balanced combination of emotions and reason, of love and truth. Neither should totally rule you. Listen to your heart and listen to your head. If they are not saying the same thing, don't make any major decisions or commitments. Wait until both your head and your heart say similar things.

Communicating your doubts about your relationship— as well as your certainties—is okay. Honestly let each know where the other stands.

Often relationships end up in the yo-yo syndrome. Just as a person playing with two yo-yos can rarely get them to be at the same level at the same time, a couple often faces a similar situation in their emotions. While one is thinking this friendship is wonderful, the other is feeling uneasy about it. After a while the reverse may be true. The person who used to be uneasy warms up to the other, and the person who was excited about the two of them cools down.

Ask Christ to get the emotional yo-yos coordinated one way or the other. Don't pressure the other person to be where you are emotionally. Be patient and allow time for change. Too often we are in a rush and end up driving the other person away.

In learning emotional closeness, give each other freedom to analyze personal feelings and to confront personal doubts.

6. Be Solution-Oriented

Ask God for wisdom regarding the other person's life. What are some of his or her needs? A good question to ask someone you are dating is, What is your most important need today? And how can I help you with it? You can't fill every need, but if your intention is to help that person mature emotionally, he or she may respond favorably and return the favor when you have needs.

An unconcerned or apathetic attitude affects the other person's emotions negatively. Think of good things that can happen. If the other person is disheartened, recognize his or her discouragement or other negative feelings and then consider together what God is likely to do to remedy the situation.

Emotional closeness involves not only sharing emotions but empathizing with each other and then helping the overburdened person find a way toward a more positive outlook. As the wise King Solomon said, "Two are better than one....For if either of them falls, the one will lift up his companion."[3]

7

Your Physical Life: Expressing Love Creatively

■ ■ ■

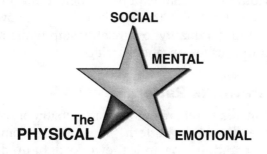

SOCIAL

MENTAL

The
PHYSICAL

EMOTIONAL

Chelsea loves her new job in a large bank. After graduating from a university in the Midwest, she settled in a major southern city and became active in the singles group of a large church. The people in the group shared Chelsea's beliefs and viewpoints about Christ and Christianity.

Because of this, Chelsea was surprised when many of the single men in the church wanted to get involved sexually on a first or second date. In fact, she discovered that many of the men and women in the group were sexually active. She was shocked to realize that so many Christians would be involved in these practices.

Chelsea shouldn't have been shocked. Everything we read and hear today—songs on the radio, TV programs, movies—all express that sexual closeness is the "ultimate"

117

experience that everyone is searching for. A minister to a single-adult church group told me that 70 percent of the singles who come to him for counsel are sexually active.

Singles encounter many physical and sexual dilemmas today. The initial interest in a person usually involves a romantic attraction, but that interest must broaden to include the whole person if the relationship is to be meaningful, beneficial, and satisfying. In today's world, old deterrents to sexual experience before marriage (the fear of pregnancy, society's disapproval, and pressure from family and friends) have been replaced by birth control, a society that encourages sexual experience before marraige, and weak family ties. All of these make it hard to know how to find and build a quality love relationship while pursuing God's purposes for sex and marriage.

The Fireworks Pattern

The media bombards us with its version of real love. I call it the "fireworks pattern." A man and woman meet each other, and the romantic fireworks light up the night. They can't keep their hands off each other as sexual attraction ignites their hormones. Intense romantic feelings overcome their inhibitions and cautions. Very soon sex is the main motivator that brings them together.

Sexual fireworks fizzle fast. Sex is a very poor glue to keep people together. Now they try to relate on other levels, but they are not even friends. They crash and burn into resentment and disgust. The pain of disillusionment is enormous. Each may feel like only a body, used by the other for their selfish desires.

Where was God during all this? He had nothing to do with it. In fact, many times throughout the Bible He warns us to stay away from sex outside marriage. Some of God's strongest prohibitions are directed at premarital sex. He strictly forbids it—not once, but many times. Such verses as

1 Corinthians 6:9-10, Galatians 5:19-21, Ephesians 5:3-7, Colossians 3:5, 1 Thessalonians 4:3-8, and Hebrews 13:4 all speak against sex outside marriage.

Does God hate you? Is He trying to take away your fun? Doesn't He know how exciting sex is?

Of course, God loves you. He loves you infinitely more than any human being could love you. God created our bodies and knows how our sexuality functions. He is no dummy. He is infinitely wise—He knows a lot more about life than you and I do.

Why reserve sex just for marriage? Because God values you so very much as a person. When you have been deeply involved with someone else through physical intimacies and intercourse, you have given away something of your being that you can never get back again. You can give away your virginity to only one person. Then, if that individual leaves your life physically and emotionally, something of you goes, too. That's why you try to build a wall around your heart to protect what's left of it.

Biblical Teaching on Immorality

Several words in the Bible are used to describe sexual immorality. One is the word "adultery." Most people believe this word refers to one or both people in a sexual situation being married to someone else. However, the biblical word is more general than that. It can mean either premarital or extramarital sex, immorality, or promiscuity. In the Bible, adultery often refers to sexual contact whether either party is married to someone else or not. It is used a number of ways in the New Testament, but it always means sexual intercourse outside the marriage bonds.

The word "fornication" usually refers to sex with someone who is not married. Some of the strongest statements in the Bible are against fornication. It is never right under any circumstances, even if the couple is in love and planning to marry. God makes this very clear.

> Do you not know that the unrighteous will not inherit the kingdom of God? Do not be deceived; neither fornicators, nor idolaters, nor adulterers, nor effeminate [by perversion], nor homosexuals, nor thieves, nor the covetous, nor drunkards, nor revilers, nor swindlers, will inherit the kingdom of God.[1]

This statement leaves no room for excuses or rationalizations. The very next verse, however, holds out hope. "Such were some of you; but you were washed, but you were sanctified, but you were justified in the name of the Lord Jesus Christ, and in the Spirit of our God."[2]

In other words, none of these wrongdoers will inherit the kingdom of God unless they have submitted their lives to God and received His forgiveness and cleansing. Many of the people attending the church located in the ancient city of Corinth had participated in one or more of these evil actions. But when they sought God's forgiveness for their evil ways, He accepted them, changed their lives, gave them salvation, sanctified them (purified their lives), and placed the Holy Spirit in their hearts to empower them to live lives that please God.

These verses show that any type of immorality, including premarital or extramarital sex, is wrong. God, in essence, says, "I don't want that to be part of your life—period." These warnings are established by God to prevent humanity, those created in His image, from becoming like animals. Sex is far more than just a physical activity to human beings, God's highest creation. Sex is a wonderful activity in the context of marriage—a relationship of total life-sharing—when God brings a man and a woman together in the security of a commitment that lasts until death separates them.

Those who have given away their virginity outside of marriage and wish they hadn't can still have hope for the future. God can cleanse you of past sin—emotionally, mentally, and spiritually. You can start on a new track of sexual purity and reserve yourself from now on for that person God will bring into your life. You can never be a physical virgin again. However, if God has cleansed you, you can develop emotional and spiritual virginity that you can keep and then give away when God leads you into a lifetime marital commitment. What a prized gift!

Getting God's perspective about physical involvement in a relationship is an important and critical part of developing oneness. It must parallel the degree of commitment that both people have to the relationship using the biblical guidelines explained later in this chapter. And both parties should understand what meaning each of them gives to their affection.

Men Communicate Physically

"Men give love to get sex and women give sex to get love." This saying may be a generalization, but it indicates the areas of our temptations.

Men often communicate more physically than verbally. We men are very competitive physically and like challenges. If a line is set that we're not supposed to cross, we're going to try to cross it just as Adam did when God set a boundary for him.

Therefore, in a relationship, a man is tempted to get too physical too soon. He is attracted to her looks, and his desires for a woman are very strong. We are made with this mechanism, and God wants us men to appreciate the women He has designed. But we must not cross the line between appreciation and sexual lust. This is why a man needs God to help him to control the drives that can entice him and to set boundaries when relating to a woman.

Women Communicate Emotionally

Many women, on the other hand, communicate more emotionally. Men may want physical involvement too soon, but women are likely to give away their hearts too soon. Women often dream and fantasize, not so much about what it would be like to have sex with a man they've just met, but what it would be like to experience romantic tenderness and closeness with him, usually within the context of a close relationship. She needs the Lord to help her control her imaginations and her vulnerability to be deceived. This was Eve's downfall.

From the very onset of their relationship, the man and woman need to know where each other is coming from. That first kiss may have a different meaning for each of them. Have you ever, either before or after kissing, asked a date what a kiss means to him or her? Probably not. It seems presumptuous and might be embarrassing to find out. Nevertheless, you need to know beforehand what a kiss is likely to mean to the other person.

I say to men, "Learn to say 'I love you' in a nonsexual manner. Become a lover in the true sense of the word—love a woman with the purity and power of God." The apostle Paul said, "Having thus a fond affection for you, we were well-pleased to impart to you not only the gospel of God but also our own lives, because you had become very dear to us."[3] Seek to do what is best for other people, and particularly for the opposite sex, as you develop a caring, committed relationship. Learn to give your heart away slowly—only within the context of developing a balanced Relationship Star. Come out from behind your emotional wall to relate more verbally and more expressively.

Women relate to feelings. They possess some sort of invisible emotional antennae. Many a man has had a woman pick up on his feelings before he knew what they were himself. A woman can sense that he's down when he himself doesn't realize it or when he doesn't want the woman to know it. The closer you get to a woman emotionally, the more she picks up on these feelings.

She may come on too strong when a man shows a little bit of interest in her. She may jump to conclusions about his intentions far too soon. Sometimes women need to slow down the process of assuming what is in men's hearts. Instead, if you like a particular man, pray that God will encourage him to open up his heart to you. Ask God to motivate him to develop your relationship. Be careful, however, not to manipulate, nor to rearrange things to control a man so that you get what you want from him. Be patient. Trust God to increase the man's attraction to you.

Talk About It

When Paula and I started dating, I was attracted to her. Although I wasn't in love with her at the time, the idea of expressing this caring in a physical manner seemed to be the natural thing to do. Based on my experience in previous relationships, I wanted to put my arm around her, kiss her, and hold her close.

Whenever I would move close to her in the car, however, I noticed that she would become quiet and seemingly disinterested. One night she sensed that I was going to put my arm around her and try to kiss her for the first time.

She then told me that she had been thinking about this possibility and wanted to talk. We were both embarrassed to bring up romantic desires and actions in conversation.

As she searched for the right words, she told me that she was having a lot of fun and thoroughly enjoyed spending time with me. "But I've learned some hard lessons from dating other men," she said. "I care for you, but at this point, I really don't want to become involved romantically. I would appreciate it if you didn't kiss me or hold my hand because if you do I'm afraid my heart and emotions will get easily confused. I have a tendency to let my heart get ahead of my head.

"I was in another relationship," she continued, "where we developed the romantic side of the relationship too quickly. When we broke up, I realized that I did not really love him. I was in love with the idea of marriage. So I would appreciate it if we didn't kiss or even hold hands until we are much closer to developing a committed relationship."

You can imagine my reaction. I was frustrated and upset. How else was I going to express my caring for her? I thought what she had asked me to do was impossible! I went home that night and told God that I couldn't do it. How could I continue to date Paula without showing some physical expression of caring for her? I simmered over the idea of not being able to hold her hand or kiss her.

As I prayed about it, however, I realized that my attention was in the wrong place. I was focusing on the sacrifices that I was making rather than on building up Paula, giving to her, and meeting her particular desires and needs. So I decided to do what she had asked. Until we had a deeper, committed relationship, I would not hold her hand or kiss her. Talk about needing the power of God—I really did! Day after day I asked the Lord for strength, wisdom, and creatvity in building my friendship with Paula.

To my amazement, it soon became exciting to realize how I could develop other areas of our relationship. This stipulation forced me to think of ways I could love Paula and show her, without physical contact, that I cared for her. It took a lot of creativity, but as a result, our relationship really blossomed.

In previous relationships, I often would get myself into trouble. It was easy for me to get romantic too soon and then feel frustrated and discouraged about the relationship never working out. Eventually, either the woman or I would break it off.

This time was unique. I was determined to put Christ first and allow Him to use each of us to show the other how to love creatively. If there was any possibility of our getting together, I wanted her to understand from her heart, her head, her spirit, and her whole being that I was the one. At this point, I didn't know if I was the one, but I certainly wanted to find out.

Nonsexual Closeness

As the level of commitment grows toward engagement and marriage, there should be some development of affection. But both persons need to know what that development means to the other. Of course, God always reserves sexual touching and intercourse for marriage—when you are committed to each other for life. Yet physical affection is a wonderful thing in a dating relationship. To hug, to run your fingers through the other person's hair, to pat the other person on the back—these are all wonderful signs of affection. We should have controlled freedom, but not license, to love creatively under God.

Women enjoy physical contact and touching with a man they like and enjoy. It can't be forced or superficial. Often, however, men misinterpret an openness to closeness and body contact from a woman as an invitation to have more intimate contact. This is why each person needs to set Christ-honoring boundaries. Don't violate each other. Communicate your convictions based on God's Word. Focus on the nonsexual closeness, companionship, and friendship that you share. As Romans 12:9 says, "Let love be without hypocrisy."

God's Principles for Loving

While the Bible says that sexual intercourse is to be confined to marriage, we still have the question, How far do you go? Yes, we should not become involved in premarital sex, but how close to it can we get?

Singles in Bible times didn't have these problems. In those days, Mom and Dad often chose a spouse for their children. Many times, the bride and groom never met until they married. Needless to say, there was very little physical contact of any kind prior to marriage. (Of course there were prostitutes, but most people had very little physical contact with the opposite sex before they married.)

The Scriptures don't specifically address our modern-day problems of how far to go in sexual intimacies, except to say that you shouldn't have intercourse before marriage. So we have to look at scriptural principles to help us determine correct sexual conduct for a single person.

Principle 1: Don't Let Anything Dominate You

> All things are lawful for me, but not all things are profitable. All things are lawful for me, but I will not be mastered by anything.[4]

This verse is part of an exhortation referring specifically to sexual conduct. "I will not be mastered by anything." So nothing, especially physical intimacy, that begins to usurp your attention and control your habits should take over your life. A Christian should not let anything but Christ dominate his or her life.

Sexual attraction is the strongest drive we have outside the survival drives (food and water, sleep, and shelter). Therefore, it is like Pandora's box. When you begin to experience some sexual intimacies, you open the lid to a lot of other things, and closing that box again can be very difficult.

Lust refers to a natural drive gone wild. When you start French kissing and sexual touching, your mind goes on ahead and your sexual urges become aroused—not only while you're with the person but at other times also. Sexual fantasizing begins to take over your mind and emotions, wherever you are, whatever you're doing. Pretty soon, the activities on a date are only a preliminary for the uncontrolled romantic activity at the end of the evenings.

Did you ever notice that the more you make out, the less you talk about significant topics? When you first start dating someone, you talk a lot, but the more you make out on dates, the shallower your verbal communication becomes and the more lopsided your Relationship Star becomes. If lust is becoming stronger in your thinking, acting, and reacting on dates, and you're talking less, then beware. God is waving a big red flag of caution. You should not come under the domination of anything except Jesus Christ.

Principle 2: Acknowledge Your Identification with Christ

> Food is for the stomach, and the stomach is for food; but God will do away with both of them. Yet the body is not for immorality, but for the Lord, and the Lord is for the body. Now God has not only raised the Lord, but will also raise us up through His power. Do you not know that your bodies are members of Christ? Shall I then take away the members of Christ and make them members of a prostitute? May it never be![5]

Paul is saying that your body is part of Christ's body. Your body belongs to Him. You are identified with Jesus Christ. He lives in you. So when you become involved in sexual intimacies, Jesus Christ is right there, too. Whether you want to believe it or not, you are bringing Christ into that immoral activity. The Lord is for the body, and the body is for the Lord.

When you go on a date and know you are going to become sexually involved, where do you usually want God? At home. Or, at least, in the trunk of the car. But when a Christian brings his or her body together with another person, God is right there with them.

One of the greatest emotional highs you can know on earth is to come together with your wife or husband in marriage and to know that God smiles on that because He has brought you together and made you one flesh. That is why, when you go too far sexually before marriage, you try to cover it up. You don't want God to be around. Have you ever played Christian music while passionately making out? Probably not. Acknowledging before you go on a date that your bodies are the Lord's will really help you control your drives and desires.

Principle 3: Flee Immorality

> Or do you not know that the one who joins himself to a prostitute is one body with her? For He says, "The two shall become one flesh." But the one who joins himself to the Lord is one spirit with Him. Flee immorality. Every other sin that a man commits is outside the body, but the immoral man sins against his own body.[6]

When we sin by committing sexual immorality, we sin against our own bodies. I don't know everything that means, but let's consider some of its meaning.

First, *you risk your health.* Recently a woman working in a Christian ministry came to me and said that she had been sexually involved with a man and now has an STD (sexually trasmitted disease). It will be with her the rest of her life. STDs ravage the body and may even cause sterility in a woman. No bodily function is safe from their attack.

Second, *you develop habits.* When a person leaves your life, you still continue the habit pattern of sexual immorality, which is likely to be carried over to the next person you date.

Third, *you get excited about the forbidden.* It's the idea that you crave what you should not have. Your body gets turned on from the excitement of the premarital sex, but what happens when you get married? The excitement leaves. One of the greatest problems in marriage today is boredom with sex. The more you mess around with sex before marriage, the less exciting it is after the wedding. Before marriage, your body reacts excitedly to the forbidden experience of premarital sex. When you marry and take the "forbidden fruit" idea out of sex and heavy sexual touching, you take out much of the excitement. You've conditioned yourself to look for the wrong kind of excitement in sex. Because your conscience has been seared by immoral behavior, you may be tempted to get into Internet pornography or other deviant sexual activity.

Principle 4: Glorify God in Your Body

> Or do you not know that your body is a temple of the Holy Spirit who is in you, whom you have from God, and that you are not your own? For you have been bought with a price: therefore glorify God in your body.[7]

Again, I don't totally understand what "glorify God in your body" means. But it does include the idea of doing holy things—things that edify and build up. When you lust a lot or are involved in heavy premarital sexual touching and intercourse, you feel guilty. The more you become involved, the colder you get toward God. You don't want to read the Bible. You rationalize your activities.

You don't want to communicate with God because He sees what you are doing in a different way than you do. You also get cold toward other believers. Who wants to worship the Lord when you feel guilty? Premarital sexual involvement drives you further away from each other instead of bringing you closer together.

In college, when we were talking about this idea, a woman told me, "When I get married and make love with my husband, I want to be able to pray at the same time." You may laugh at that idea, but I thought it was beautiful. Think about that. Seriously. Just to have the smile of God on a marriage relationship and to know that He is right there with you and your spouse is worth the world. No hiding. Sexual enjoyment in the context of a committed, loving marriage is encouraged and blessed by God. That is real excitement!

Principle 5: Control Your Passions

> For this is the will of God, your sanctification [which means to make you holy or set apart for Him]; that is, that you abstain from sexual immorality; that each of you know how to possess his own vessel [his body] in sanctification and honor, not in lustful passion, like the Gentiles [non-Christians] who do not know God.[8]

So, Paul says, choose activities that are wholesome and honorable. That is, discipline your passions so that you participate in activities that enhance your relationship with the Lord. Just because friends, TV shows, movies, and books say promiscuity is okay doesn't mean you should get involved in immorality. Strive to be pure in your thoughts and actions. That's God's will for you. The Bible is the guidebook for living the best life.

Principle 6: Don't Defraud

> ...and that no man transgress and defraud his brother in the matter because the Lord is the avenger in all these things, just as we also told you before and solemnly warned you. For God has not called us for the purpose of impurity, but in sanctification. So, he who rejects this is not rejecting man but the God who gives His Holy Spirit to you.[9]

This is an important principle. The word "defraud" means to inflame someone's passions without being able to righteously fulfill them. In essence, you are giving the other person a false lead. Our bodies are designed somewhat like the standard transmission of a car. After you start a car, you put it into first gear. When you speed up, you shift into second gear, then third, and finally fourth. The car is constructed in a way that allows you to start a process and reach your destination.

Our bodies have a similar process. God designed sexual foreplay to lead to intercourse within the boundaries of a committed, loving, marital union. When you start foreplay, your mind and body move forward toward the natural conclusion of the sexual act. Defrauding means to get the emotional, sexual engine going inside of the other person without being able to arrive at the righteous destination God intended, which is sexual intercourse between a husband and wife who are bound together in God's love.

Some people who want to follow biblical commands and yet are caught up in the current emphasis on sexual freedom may ask, Does intercourse mean only the penetration of a man into a woman? After one of my seminars,

Jeff wanted to know if it was all right to engage in sexual touching and oral sex just as long as it did not include the physical entering of a man into a woman.

I use a term for this kind of behavior: "sexual outercourse." It means doing everything possible except sexual intercourse. Many people think participating in sexual outercourse is okay because they still remain a virgin. They haven't committed the big no-no.

Jesus Christ put thinking like this on a different level. In Matthew 5:27-28 He said, "You have heard that it was said, 'You shall not commit adultery'; but I say to you that everyone who looks at a woman with lust for her has already committed adultery with her in his heart." Not only the physical act but also the mental images that come to mind are wrong. Christ took the emphasis away from just the physical and put it into the realm of the mental activity that occurs before the physical.

When Jeff told me that he could lie naked with his girlfriend and sexually touch her without having intercourse, I explained to him that he had violated God's prohibition. If you are unmarried and participate in sexual outercourse, you have defrauded each other and committed adultery according to Christ.

If you have a hard time with the temptation to defraud someone, don't start up the engine in the first place. What starts up your engine? Holding hands? Front-to-front hugs? French kissing? Sexual touching? Whenever your sexual desires are aroused, stop the internal motor before you go too far mentally as well as physically.

Some ask, Who should stop the process, the man or the woman? If you have trouble in this area, why don't the two of you seek God's direction together before the date? Seek His guidance as to what you should do and how you should behave.

Emery, a recent university graduate, said that he makes it a habit to ask the Holy Spirit for guidance before he and his girlfriend go out on a date. He does so not necessarily to guard himself from doing something wrong, but because, as he said, "I want to know how to authentically and purely communicate my affection to her in words and deeds."

Did you ever notice that when you're involved with someone, you want to have sex, but you don't want to? You like it, but you don't like it. When you experience confusion, emptiness, frustration, or guilt, you are defrauding the other person. A major reason why couples break up is that they have become too close sexually before marriage.

Principle 7: Pursue Purity

> Flee from youthful lusts and pursue righteousness, faith, love and peace, with those who call on the Lord from a pure heart.[10]

If your desires are leading into activities that displease God, stop immediately. Don't stay there and think, "I know I've got to get out of this situation soon." Don't wait for "soon." Get out of there immediately!

Remember the old analogy about putting a frog in a pot of water? Put it in when the pot is boiling, and the frog immediately jumps right back out again. However, put it in when the water is cold, and he will enjoy it. Then turn up the heat ever so slowly, and the frog will stay in the water, relaxing as it gets warmer. He will stay in the pot until he boils to death.

Sharing sexual intimacies is like that. Don't wait until you feel you're reaching the point of no return. It's too late. Better yet, don't get into the pot even when the water is cold. Look at the consequences of your activities. If you don't want to get involved in sinful behavior, stop the process before it starts. Find out what constitutes the pot for you and stay away from it. Here are some suggestions for avoiding wrong activities:

- If you don't want to end up making out with your girlfriend in a lonely spot, decide to go to a restaurant instead.

- If you don't want to end up getting physically involved when your boyfriend comes to your home and you sit on the sofa watching TV, sit around the kitchen table instead. Or better yet, go for a walk.

You're right, these suggestions aren't romantic. That's the idea! Remember, if you marry this person, most of your time with him or her will be in an unromantic environment. If you wonder how you will respond in the everyday circumstances of married life, then following similar suggestions will help provide an answer.

If you have had problems in the area of physical intimacy before, tell the Lord that you have learned your lesson. Accept His forgiveness and trust Him for His power to lead a holy life.

Controlling Your Sexual Desires

How do you start to control your sexual desires? Often this is the area of our biggest battles and greatest questions. Because I was single for 42 years, I know about these struggles firsthand. Here are the principles God taught me during those years.

1. Admit You Have Sex Drives

When I was single, I used to pray that God would take away my sexual desires because the sexual temptations I constantly faced often seemed overwhelming. After asking God for years, it suddenly dawned on me one day that I was asking the Lord to neuter me. I am thankful for unanswered prayers! If God had answered my requests, I would not be married today.

Have you sometimes tried to deny your drives while all the time you were a roaring lion underneath?

Be encouraged. God is the one who gives us an interest in the opposite sex and can help us control our drives. Why deny our God-given interests or ask Him to remove them? However, we should remember the difference between interest and lust. I think the greatest creation of God is a woman. I don't know of anything else that rivals her for first place. But you can appreciate the opposite sex without lusting.

2. Submit Your Sexual Desires to God

Keep giving your sexual desires to the Lord. Christ said the greatest commandments are to love the Lord your God with all your heart, soul, and mind and to love your neighbor as yourself.[11]

When you can't fulfill your sexual desire in a righteous manner, then love God more. Have a passion to know Jesus Christ to a greater extent. Trust Him for power—He is the only one who can give you control. "Discipline yourself for the purpose of godliness ... [which] is profitable for all things, since it holds promise for the present life and also for the life to come."[12]

So when sexual desires crowd into your thoughts, turn them over to the Lord and ask Him for the power and the courage to control your passions.

3. Keep Your Mind Pure

Finally, brothers, whatever is true, whatever is noble, whatever is right, whatever is pure, whatever is lovely, whatever is admirable—if anything is excellent or praiseworthy—think about such things.[13]

The conversations you have, the magazine pictures you look at, the TV programs you watch, and the books you read all have a tendency to inflame your mind. When you fill your mind with all the sexuality and sensuality of the world, it's no wonder you have problems controlling your thoughts and actions.

The computer world uses an acronym: GIGO. That stands for "Garbage In, Garbage Out." You put misinformation into your computer and that's what comes out. Your mind works the same way. You fill it with garbage, and that's what you will think about and do. Change GIGO. to mean "God In, God Out." Remember this: You are the only guardian of your mind. No one else is going to protect your thought life. Fill your mind with Scripture and wholesome things, and the Holy Spirit will use those good things to give you moral victories.

4. Channel Your Energies

Let God channel this deep-seated power of wanting to love somebody toward a desire to help other people. This is what kept me going for many years. Take opportunities to give love to all kinds of needy people. Exhaust yourself in furthering God's message of love and salvation throughout your world.

Here is a radical statement that I wholeheartedly believe: God is so creative that He can satisfy your sexual desires even without sex. He did that in my life.

5. Develop Friendships with the Opposite Sex

Sometimes, if you're not dating, all you want to do is talk to someone of the opposite sex. You want to know something about how the other half of the world lives. Aren't they a mystery?

I say again, begin to develop good, deep friendships with people of the opposite sex. Don't limit this to people you are interested in romantically, but include people who can be good, dependable friends. Take the initiative to be friendly. When you are lonely, the tendency is to withdraw. Do the opposite. Get a group of people together and have a good time. By the way, you probably won't lust after a friend you respect.

6. Build a Support Group

Start a CELL group. The letters are an acronym meaning Christians Encouraging, Loving, Learning. Men, get a group of men. Women, get a group of women. Choose people with whom you really want to become "blood" brothers or sisters. Pour your souls out together. Uphold each other in prayer. But in order to do that, you must know what the other persons' needs are.

Be accountable to each other for your attitudes and actions. Ask the hard questions that will keep you close to the biblical standard of living and relating. Ask the others to pray for you while you are on a date or while you are home alone. Afterward, they should ask you, "What did you do on your date or when you were alone? Did you do anything that would displease the Lord?"

The last question should always be, "Have you just told us any lies?"

Tuning Your Life

Sex is similar to tuning an orchestra. In a symphony orchestra, you have many fine, delicate instruments. You have the woodwinds, including the oboe, the clarinet, the flute, and the bassoon. You have the stringed instruments—

violins, violas, cellos, and basses. You have the brass—trumpets, trombones, French horns, and tubas. You have the percussion, including cymbals, bells, and various drums. If you're playing *The 1812 Overture,* you also have a few cannons on stage.

You usually tune an orchestra by the oboe. As the first oboist tunes and then repeatedly plays one note, the whole orchestra tunes their instruments to that same tone. But what if the bass drum player decided he wanted to tune the orchestra? The bass drum would blast out in tremendous booms that would drown out all those delicate instruments.

Sex is similar to that. It is the second greatest drive in our lives. Once we become involved in it, it has the tendency to overpower all those fine, delicate areas of our Relationship Star—the social, mental, emotional, and spiritual areas of life.

We have to realize that the physical area of a relationship needs to be in coordination with the other areas of our lives and, in particular, with the commitment level of the other individual in the relationship. Mutual commitment to develop oneness under God's direction is critically important.

So remember to enjoy one another, to bear each other's burdens, to pursue godliness, and always to walk closely with the Lord Jesus.

8

Your Spiritual Life: Exploring Your Souls

■ ■ ■

When Paula and I were in Paris, we visited Le Louvre Museum and spent hours looking at its beautiful paintings and art objects. A large crowd of people stood in front of one painting, blocking our view. As people moved on, we got closer and saw that the painting was the famous Mona Lisa. We had seen copies in books and magazines, but here was the original, the masterpiece created by Leonardo da Vinci. We stood captivated by its beauty and elegance.

God is an artist and originator, too, infinitely greater than da Vinci. God is the creative genius not only of the material world but also of relationships. Even in the Garden of Eden, God said about Adam, "It is not good for the man to be alone."[1] He decided to create Eve so that Adam could have a companion and a deep oneness with another being similar to himself.

139

As the architect of relationships, God knows all the intricacies of building a beautiful original. Far more than just giving you an original to copy, He has given you guidelines for developing your own unique marital relationship, one that will satisfy you for a lifetime.

Spiritual Goals for Dating

A good marriage is built upon the character values, experiences, and attitudes that each person brings into their marital union. The quality of a dating relationship, and later a marriage, depends upon the quality of each person's personal life and spiritual walk with Jesus Christ.

In the Scriptures, God gives us His beautiful, original design for the marriage relationship, the ultimate in intimate relating. This design brings a husband and wife a tight-knit oneness. As we study the original design, we can see how to build a dating relationship into one of close, intimate commitment.

God gives us a quality in our associations with others that we can never attain by ourselves. To accomplish this, He has given the Holy Spirit as helper, assistant, guide, and source of power. Without the Holy Spirit, we could never develop anything close to what God has to offer us. He is the master teacher and leader of relationships.

We must admit that marriage is in trouble today. The escalating divorce rate, the growing number of abused wives and children, and the increase in marital unhappiness, isolation, and frustration all show that to be true. This is not because God's original design is wrong but because human copies and imitations of it are nowhere near what God intended for us.

Many different ideas about relationships are espoused by books, movies, television, etc. Some time ago a famous movie star appeared on television explaining the joy of having a baby outside marriage. She had lived with her lover, the father of her child, for five years, but still didn't plan to marry him. Such ideas broadcast widely by the media affect the lives of many people who say, "Well, if that star can do it, then I can, too." Yet years later, the media revealed the wreckage of that relationship.

Down through the ages, when people have said, "I have a better way; I know how to build a better relationship," they inevitably have found out differently. Anything but God's design is a cheap imitation.

In the past, children were reared with Judeo-Christian principles of living, which included guidelines for relationships. By the time a person married, he or she knew enough to stick to their vows of "till death do us part." Divorce was a rare event. Today, when ungodly ideals permeate our society and world, perhaps most people, even Christian singles, have not learned before marriage how to build a quality marriage relationship that will last a lifetime.

Walking down the aisle in the wedding ceremony does not change weak values or character into good marriage traits. Before marriage is the time to build the qualities that will foster a good relationship, not just for one or two years but for a lifetime.

Dating Goal 1: Building Spiritual Oneness

Right after God created Eve, He told Adam, "For this reason a man shall leave his father and his mother, and be joined to his wife; and they shall become one flesh."[2] When Christ was on earth, He quoted that statement and then added these words to it: "So they are no longer two, but one flesh. What therefore God has joined together, let no man separate."[3]

The first step toward marriage oneness is to *leave*. You leave your parents or anyone else on whom you've been dependent for emotional, mental, or material needs or guidance. You're called to love, honor, and respect your parents, but when you marry, you are to leave dependency on them and all others behind and learn to be interdependent with and responsible to your spouse. Continued dependency on parents and relatives can be a major problem for newly married couples. Certainly, seeking the friendship and counsel of others outside the marriage is a good idea, but the final decisions should be made between spouses who now take responsibility for their own lives together. Learn to lean on each other.

The husband and wife take the second step toward spiritual oneness when they *cleave* to each other. This word means to stick like glue, signifying the lasting commitment a husband and wife have made to each other. If, when you walk down the aisle at your wedding ceremony, you do it with the attitude, "I hope this works," it probably won't. Complications and difficulties will disintegrate your marriage if you have a "hope so" attitude.

I was speaking to a large high school convention. During my presentation, I mentioned that when I asked Paula to marry me, I told her, "Honey, once we walk down the aisle in marriage, the only way out of our relationship is if you die or I die. We have no other choice." Suddenly, 900 students erupted in applause and cheering.

This shocked me. Apparently, many of them came from broken or loveless homes. What these students desired deep in their souls was a strong family relationship where mother and father deeply loved each other and cleaved to each other through thick and thin, in good times and bad.

Cleaving includes a unique loyalty between a man and woman that says, "Our home is a refuge against the world and the winds of change." Even in a dating relationship, you can develop a sense of commitment that, if the relationship results in marriage, will build to a sense of cleaving. From the beginning, you can develop a mental commitment, even for just that one date. Be careful when you go out with someone to make sure that you don't have wandering eyes all evening, focusing on anyone else who looks interesting. Instead, you can focus on that one person who is your date, thinking how you can be of help and encouragement to him or her just for that evening.

As your relationship grows increasingly serious, develop higher levels of commitment. When I became engaged to Paula, the question kept coming back to my mind over and over again, "In what ways can I commit myself to her for a lifetime? I have seen so many relationships disintegrate and fail. How can I develop a commitment to her that is not going to break apart over the years?"

Finally, I realized that God is the only one who knows the future as well as the present. If He was guiding me to marry Paula, then He was the one who would give me the ability to commit myself to her for the rest of my life. Christ committed Himself to us forever, and He knows what commitment is all about. As I align myself with His heart, He will give me the sustaining commitment that I desperately need.

The third step toward spiritual oneness is becoming *one flesh*. This means that two individuals merge together into a single, unique unit. They don't lose their individuality. They are not submerged into the whole relationship. Rather, their individuality is enhanced by being a part of each other.

Some people interpret "one flesh" to mean a woman joins a man on his life's path. Others believe it means the man joins the woman on her life's path. For others, it means both keep their individual paths, which happen to meet on occasion.

None of these is correct. Rather, a unique woman and a unique man on two different paths of life come together to forge a third path. The merger is a new relationship, unique in every way, so that the third road is something totally new to both of them. Never before has this particular road been traveled. This new road helps fill out both of their personalities and characters. It is a lifelong path of discovery, enjoyment, and adventure in becoming one.

Obviously, the physical consummation of a lifetime commitment in marriage is sexual intercourse. However, being of one flesh is represented not just by intercourse. That is a sign of it, but oneness is also the merging together of two unique people into a harmonious, mutually enriching relationship.

In dating, we work toward a balanced and harmonious Relationship Star. The physical attractions and desires are placed in God's hands to be the final consummation after the commitment of marriage has been made publicly before God and others.

Building oneness requires that you and the person you are dating become students of each other. Learn how to build harmony by discovering how to enhance each other's personality and strengths and minimize your weaknesses. Discover where you are needed in the other person's life to strengthen weak areas and to complete the person.

Dating Goal 2: Becoming Spirit-Filled

> And do not get drunk with wine, for that is dissipation, but be filled with the Spirit, speaking to one another in psalms and hymns and spiritual songs, singing and making melody with your heart to the Lord; always giving thanks for all things in the name of our Lord Jesus Christ to God, even the Father; and be subject to one another in the fear of Christ.[4]

To be Spirit-filled is to have a daily dependence upon and trust in the Holy Spirit. According to Scripture, the Spirit of God is the third person of the Trinity and the source of daily power—not just in a marriage but in the whole of our lives. If we are Christians, then the Holy Spirit is inside us. You can activate the Spirit's power in you by asking Him in faith to fill you moment by moment. Becoming Spirit-reliant instead of self-reliant releases His power and guidance for our lives.

Learn how to be filled with the Holy Spirit by faith and to experience all the power, joy, and love that the Spirit can bring.

The Spirit of God affects our values, behavior, and attitudes. A Spirit-filled attitude is one that gives thanks for all things, even when the going gets tough and the circumstances seem difficult. The Spirit-filled attitude also includes being subject to other Christians in the fear of Christ, realizing that we are to be subject first to Him and second to each other. The key to a harmonious relationship is being humble, respecting each other's opinions and thoughts and honoring one another before the Lord.

When I told Paula that I loved her and wanted her to be my wife, I told her she would always be second in my life. Jesus Christ would be first. If Paula were to be first in my life, I could not personally generate the consistent love that she should receive. Only as Christ energizes me and motivates me, providing His love for Paula through me, can she receive all the love that she needs.

And Paula does not put me first in her life. She gets her strength and fulfillment first from God Himself. Should either of us put the other first, then the other becomes that person's god. Jesus Christ must be God of all and overflow His love through each of us to the other through His Holy Spirit.

Through a Spirit-filled walk with Christ, we build toward maturity in relationships as He molds and develops our character. As we trust Jesus Christ, we learn to be subject to and humble toward each other. When differences come into a relationship, we confront them not by arguing in a spirit of contentiousness but by being humble, kind, and gentle toward each other.

Dating Goal 3: Building Biblical Attitudes

In the book of Ephesians, right after the apostle Paul admonishes us to be filled with the Spirit of God, he begins to write about the marriage relationship. He says:

Husbands ought also to love their own wives as their own bodies. He who loves his own wife loves himself; for no one ever hated his own flesh, but nourishes and cherishes it, just as Christ also does the church, because we are members of His body....This mystery is great; but I am speaking with reference to Christ and the church.[5]

The Man's Responsibility

In marriage, the man is commanded by God to love his wife with a love represented by the love Jesus had for the church—the people for whom He sacrificed Himself and died. Why did He sacrifice Himself? So that He could sanctify the church—set it apart and elevate it above all else. This is the same type of love that a husband ought to have for his wife. This kind of love must come, first of all, through submission to Jesus Christ.

My understanding of this passage is that the man ultimately holds the responsibility of the home. He is to set the standard and be the leader and protector of the home. When decisions are to be made, he consults with his wife and interacts with her on various possibilities. In the final analysis, however, he is accountable to God for the decision that they make.

Even while dating, a man can develop the leadership abilities needed in marriage. He needs to learn to choose what is best for the relationship in order to give security to the woman. Putting her needs above his own will teach him to become a servant-leader, one who leads by serving. One of the great lessons of life is to love consistently, not just when everything is fine, the emotions are flowing, and romance is in the air. A couple's love for each other should flow even when life is uninspiring, routine, and dull, and even when there have been misunderstandings or periods of silence. Remember, love seeks the highest and best for the other person. Become a student of the Scriptures—to find and follow God's path above all else—in order to develop these characteristics.

In a dating relationship, however, a man should remember that he is not married to the woman. Therefore, he does not have to commit himself to her totally or sacrifice everything for her. Don't act married before you are married. Ask penetrating questions of yourself and of God so that you will discover His will concerning whether you are to be together or not. Remember that in marriage, both the husband and the wife are to "be subject to one another in the fear of Christ."[6]

That means to be humble, to respect each other, and to develop mutual harmony. If you are moving toward marrying your girlfriend, do you sense a growing desire to lovingly lead and serve her? Is she pleased with your leadership?

The Woman's Responsibility

In a marriage relationship, a wife is to "be subject to [her] own husband as to the Lord."[7] As she has given herself to Christ, a wife should give herself to her husband. She must understand that humility and direction are ultimately from Christ, not from her husband. Christ provided an environment where He laid down His life for the church, and the church responded in love, understanding, and subjection. Even so, the husband is to provide that kind of environment and atmosphere in which the wife can joyfully respond in gratitude and respect.

In such a home, persons are equal and yet function uniquely. Male and female barriers are broken down. The apostle Paul wrote, "There is neither Jew nor Greek, there is neither slave nor free man, there is neither male nor female; for you are all one in Christ Jesus."[8] The woman is not more important than the man, nor the man more important than the woman. They are equally loved and valued by God. Both must treat each other in the same way.

While dating, a woman should be discerning about her boyfriend's character and abilities to lead and make difficult decisions. She is not held to the "be subject" command.

In dating, the woman needs to learn to respect the man and to respond to him as he tries to provide an atmosphere of love and acceptance. You cannot respond to a person you don't deeply respect, so build that confidence in him. Do you find yourself pulling him down or picking him apart? Be careful not to be contentious but to encourage and build him up. A woman, as well as a man, must trust God to choose a good spouse. How do you know He is guiding you toward marriage?

The Decision-Making Process

After Paula and I became engaged, we went for premarital counseling with a Christian psychologist. After reviewing the personality tests he had given us, he made an interesting observation. He noticed that I am a very objective person. I see facts and figures and come up with what I believe are logical conclusions. My score was the highest you can get in this regard, at the very top of the scale of objectivity. Paula's score, on the other hand, showed that she is far more subjective in her reasoning. Her score was in the normal range between subjectivity and objectivity.

Then the psychologist made this statement, "Dick, when it comes to making decisions and seeing circumstances as they truly are, you think you will be correct. But most of the time Paula will be right." That killed me! I did not want to believe that. Yet, after many years of marriage, I can say the statement is absolutely true. I have learned to depend upon her wisdom and insights. Only two times in our marriage have I made major decisions for our family without considering Paula's perspective. Both of those incidents are etched in my memory because in each situation, my unilateral decision proved to be wrong.

Encouraging Each Other

In dating, a woman should help to develop a harmonious spirit in the relationship. Learn how to encourage your boyfriend and to point him to the Lord Jesus and the Scriptures. Develop a spirit of cooperation regarding decisions you make as a couple. Do you sense a growing oneness in your decision-making process?

If a woman feels put down or squelched, she may want to look for another man. She should feel free to discuss her thoughts openly and freely with her boyfriend and give her opinions without being looked down upon or belittled. Do you both affirm each other?

It greatly encourages me when Paula says over and over, "I believe in you, Dick. I know you can do it." Such words would not mean nearly as much if I didn't have confidence in her opinions and her love for the Lord.

A woman should develop a confidence in God and experience His peace—that gentle and quiet spirit that comes from being filled with His Holy Spirit. We are all commanded to submit to one another. But the unique form of respect of a wife toward her husband is found only in the marriage relationship. It doesn't refer to a woman who is dating a man. If your boyfriend doesn't provide for you an atmosphere of acceptance, commitment, wholesome morality, and godliness, you should be skeptical about his integrity. Choose a man with qualities you honestly admire, someone to whom you can easily submit, not just a romantic lover.

The most helpful lesson Paula ever learned about submission to a husband was through a working relationship she had before we were married. For six years she worked closely with the director of the Florida State University Campus Crusade for Christ ministry. Paula was the coordinator of the women's ministry on that university campus. The director valued Paula's input, gave her responsibility for various activities, took her suggestions with a teachable spirit, and worked together with her in close harmony. Paula loved her role, but she also loved knowing that the final responsibility for everything they were doing lay with him. This gave her a great umbrella of freedom under which to work. At the same time, it took many burdens off her shoulders.

This is now the way that she and I work together in marriage. Paula is a tremendous help. We divide up responsibilities, and I love building her up as well. When we disagree regarding a decision that has to be made, she gives me her input and then relaxes as I make the final decision. Why does she relax? Because she knows that ultimately I will have to answer to God for our decisions. The buck stops with me, and she is home free. She views this as another way that God so wonderfully and masterfully designed ways to protect her.

Spiritual Guidelines for Dating

1. Commit Your Relationship to God

Realize that the burden of your relationship is not on you but on God. He is the Creator, the Lord God of the universe, the one who has all things under His control. He knows your past, present, and future, and He knows all about the person you are dating.

Too often we want to control everything ourselves. We like to believe we have the upper hand and that nothing is going to surprise us. But we are finite; the future is really a mystery to us.

The basis for a good relationship then is God's Word. His thoughts are on paper, there for you and me to know. Applying His thoughts takes the pressure off us and puts it on Him. We should allow our expectations for a dating relationship to come from Him, not from our own romantic desires.

Paula realized this after she broke up with a guy she had been dating seriously. In reading the book of Psalms she saw the words, "My soul, wait in silence for God only, for my hope is from Him."[9]

She realized that she had been putting her expectations and hopes in marriage and not in the Lord Himself. In fact, she had been trying to make it work out by her design rather than waiting on the Lord. As she started seeking His direction, He led her to break off the relationship. Three years later, when I came into her life, Paula was trusting God and enjoying her life. That's why I was so attracted to her.

2. Recognize Open Spaces and Fences

As we seek God's will, He will show us every twist and turn in the road, and He knows where that road is going. When we give a relationship to Him, He may guide us to develop and expand that relationship into a beautiful marriage commitment. But sometimes He also puts fences into a relationship and says, "Here are My limits." He pulls people apart because He knows that they are not best for each other. Not all love is meant to be married love. Even if we don't know why, God does.

When I was a senior in college, I was devastated when Ruth told me she no longer wanted to date me. All my plans were shattered. She was a wonderful woman, and I had thought we were headed toward marriage. Three years later, I was working with Campus Crusade for Christ at the University of Georgia. At Christmastime, I went home to New Jersey to visit my parents. From a friend, I learned that Ruth was now enrolled in a nursing school in New York City, a 20-minute drive from my parents' home.

On a whim, I gave her a call and asked her if she would like to go out. To my surprise, she accepted. That night, as we talked, I asked, "Do you still counsel women like you used to in college? So many women enjoyed talking with you then."

"Oh yes," she answered, "but I don't counsel like you do. You talk about Jesus Christ in your counseling, don't you?"

"Well, sure," I replied. "He's the only one who can meet people's needs."

"I don't believe that anymore," she told me. "In fact, I don't believe in God anymore. I have my boyfriend, and he is all I really believe in now."

I was stunned. She continued to downgrade God in a hostile manner. In college, when I was growing in my faith, she had been right there with me. I ended up strong for the Lord and wanting to serve Him. Unknown to me, she had gone the opposite way.

As I said good night that evening, I was very thankful to God that He had removed Ruth from my life three years previously. Her inner character was so different from what I wanted in a wife. She had chosen a different path. God knew this and saved me from becoming further committed to her. How thankful I am that God built a fence in our relationship and stopped our progress toward marriage.

3. Expect Prayer—Not Pressure—to Build Responses

Sometimes, when we really love a person, that person may not share the same level of enthusiasm we have for the relationship. When this happens, we may try to manipulate and force the other person to love us. Such manipulative pressure usually backfires. It's more likely to make a person run away than draw closer to us. Pressure causes a person to feel boxed in and controlled. Spontaneity and a sense of fun are lost.

Sometimes, of course, pressure works for a while. You may even manipulate someone to marry you. But when he or she realizes how much pressure you exerted, his or her respect for you will be lost. Instead of respecting your ability as a master-manipulator, the other person will see that you are a master-deceiver. You may get what you want instead of desiring whatever is best for the other person.

Pressure confuses a person. The person who is being pushed along doesn't know if he or she really loves you and will eventually doubt the commitment that he or she made.

Manipulation reveals that the manipulator is selfish, insecure, and afraid of losing. Otherwise, the person would have been willing for the relationship to develop freely. When we grant freedom, a relationship is more likely to be a lasting one.

When I started dating Paula, she lived in Tallahassee, Florida; I lived in San Bernardino, California—2200 miles apart. I was constantly traveling, speaking on university campuses and at conferences throughout America. Because of my lifestyle, I had quite a list of failed long-distance relationships. I had often tried to force different women to like me by pressuring them to write or call me. I used to send a woman many friendship cards, in order to remind them to communicate with me. I sent the cards to make them feel guilty if they did not correspond with me as frequently as I wished. One of my favorite cards stated, "My mailbox is hungry. It has eaten all your mail. Please send some more." After years of doing this, I became disgusted with my manipulative habits.

Then Paula came into my life. I tried not to put guilt on her. I constantly prayed that God would motivate her heart to like me. After receiving a letter from me, she would respond in nine or ten days. I could have written her back immediately. But I decided to write back at her level of interest but shorten the time slightly to show my interest. I would send a letter in seven or eight days and then a little sooner the next time. But I never wanted her to write because of guilt feelings.

I figured, if I can trust God's working in my heart and life, then I can trust Him to work in Paula's heart and life, too. The writer of Proverbs hit the nail on the head. He said, "The king's heart is like channels of water in the hand of the LORD; He turns it wherever He wishes."[10]

I reasoned that because God could change channels of water and turn a king's heart, He could turn a woman's heart to love me if this is what He wanted. Why not pray that He would motivate Paula to love me? How much better to have spontaneous love and caring than to manipulate it. Let internal motivation from God be the source of pressure. Be a person of prayer, seeking to have God's hand in the relationship.

4. Change Obstacles into Opportunities for Growth

Every couple runs into obstacles in their relationship. Strong couples will pray together about such problems, talk them out, and search the Scriptures for God's answers. Some Christians over-spiritualize their search for answers to problems. They talk to God about them but not to the other person. Others struggle with the difficulties they are having and quickly decide they are an automatic sign that God wants the relationship discontinued. They fail to see that obstacles are often opportunities for growth in the relationship. Working through obstacles is difficult, but continue with the relationship until God makes it plain that you shouldn't. Use these obstacles to develop your faith together and your commitment to each another.

In my book *A Personal Experiment in Faith-Building,*[11] I explain that faith has three ingredients: knowledge, affirmation, and reliance. *Knowledge* refers to knowing God's Word and knowing God Himself. *Affirmation* is developing a positive response to the things you learn from God's Word. *Reliance* is mixing knowledge and affirmation together to move forward, depending on God to give guidance, wisdom, and strength.

When you come across the obstacles, differences, or even annoying habits of the other person, don't get frustrated and explode. Instead, seek the Lord's guidance to handle all those things wisely. Let the obstacles motivate you to search the Scriptures, to develop stronger faith in Him, and to find that He can carry you through them.

5. Develop Spiritual Harmony

To develop together spiritually, first develop your personal relationship with Christ. Have daily communion with Him and learn to abide in Him. In your dating, discover how each of you relates to God. You don't have to think exactly alike regarding all spiritual issues. However, you both need to have a dependence upon God to guide you individually and together.

As I mentioned earlier, the Bible states very clearly that you should not date non-Christians and become romantically or emotionally involved with them. "Do not be yoked together with unbelievers. For what do righteousness and wickedness have in common? Or what fellowship can light have with darkness?...What does a believer have in common with an unbeliever?"[12]

That applies not only to marriage but also to dating because dating is the foundation for marriage. Those who are not Christians are self-reliant and not Christ-reliant. No matter how good they seem to be, their lives run contrary to God's will for your own life.

I come across many people who dated non-Christians, developed an emotional attachment, and married them. Why do Christians do this? Often I hear the following reason: "I'm strong. I can handle this." Such reasoning can be likened to two people holding hands, one standing on a table and the other on the floor, each wanting to pull the other to their own level. It's much easier for a person to be pulled down to the floor than to be pulled up onto the table. Christians are on a different plane than non-Christians because they have a spiritual dimension with God. But so often Christians compromise their walk with God in order to marry non-Christians. They pay a heavy penalty for that decision.

Another excuse I often hear is, "I'm praying that God will use me in this person's life." This is sometimes labeled "missionary dating." God may want to use you in that person's life, but on the other hand, He may not. Satan may be wanting to use that person in your life instead! When you date a non-Christian, you compromise your spiritual values and moral integrity for the relationship.

One woman told me, "Well, I love him, and God loves him, so he will change for us." Don't be fooled. Even if the person says that he or she will become a Christian, don't marry (or promise to marry) that person until the person submits themselves totally to Christ, until that person exhibits definite spiritual changes resulting from that commitment, and until he or she has had time to grow and develop their faith. Too often a Christian marries a person who promises to become a Christian or who even shows initial signs of a conversion experience, only to live the rest of their lives with someone who does not serve or love Christ.

On the other hand, should the person you are dating become a dedicated Christian and start studying the Scriptures, that person will want to know what you were doing dating him or her as a non-Christian! That person's Christian standards may end up being higher than yours, in which case your relationship is likely to break up anyway. Your refusal to date a non-Christian might have a powerful effect on the person's eventual conversion to Christ and leave a greater respect for your Christian convictions. I've known this to happen in several instances.

A similar caution applies to committed Christians dating cold or lukewarm Christians. Too often the committed Christians change, their zeal for God dies down, and their eyes are turned away from God.

Ask yourself these questions regarding the person you are dating:

- Does this individual bring out the best or the worst in me?

- Does this person have a dynamic relationship with Christ that builds me up?

- Does he or she seek God's guidance in our relationship or depend upon self?

- Do I have to prop up this person spiritually, or is he or she able to stand alone, trusting in Christ?

A relationship between two committed Christians is a beautiful thing to behold. It is blessed by God with a unique depth and joy. Yes, that couple will have differences to work with and difficulties to overcome because they are uniquely male and female, imperfect, and living in an imperfect world. But when their relationship is blessed by God, they will experience a oneness, a total life sharing, that is supernatural in origin. The saying is true: A good marriage is made in heaven.

Spiritual Activities for Dating

Sharing spiritual activities will not only bring you closer together but will also keep your eyes on the Lord, the source of strength for making your relationship a godly one.

1. Minister to One Another

Take part in one or more of the following activities depending on how long you have known or dated each other.

- Share your own spiritual thoughts and experiences, past and present.

- If you like to sing, put psalms to music, compose praise songs to the Lord, or sing along with recorded Christian music. Attend worship services together.

- Relate your spiritual heritage, including your personal testimony of how you first met Christ.

- Discuss the content of sermons, books, and tapes that you hear or read together.

- Take turns giving thanks to God before meals.

- Discuss doctrines of the faith. If you don't understand each other's beliefs, look for explanatory helps in a Christian bookstore or church library or from a pastor or other theologically trained person.

- Exchange encouraging Scriptures each day.

- Memorize Scripture verses together and repeat them to one another.

- Regularly study the Bible together, perhaps using a Bible study guide such as my book *Growing Closer to God*[13] to give you an understanding of God's principles for a successful marriage.

- Share personal spiritual battles and victories, past and present.

- Explain your goals and purposes in life and how each of you wants to glorify God.

- Write notes during personal Bible study and prayer times and later discuss these together.

- Pray together.

When praying together, be careful about hidden problems that might arise. Some couples struggle with sharing very personal feelings and intimate thoughts in prayer because it leads to a driving desire for deeper emotional and physical intimacy. I have known Christian couples who started with prayer and ended in bed together. Pray together over the phone or early in the evening rather than late at night when physical tiredness may relax moral convictions.

During the engagement period, one couple I know called each other nightly and prayed together on the phone. In this way, they developed a spiritual intimacy and foundation for their marriage without temptation.

2. Reach Out and Minister to Others Together

As your relationship develops, resist the temptation to be exclusive in your relationship. Sometimes sharing about Christ and the Christian life together is easier than doing it on your own. Consider growing spiritually as a couple by taking part together in some of the following activities with each other.

- Attend a regular Bible study.

- Lead a Bible study.

- Teach a Sunday school class.

- Visit hospital patients, retirement home residents, or other shut-ins.

- Participate in church visitation.

- Invite non-Christian couples to dinner and share Christ with them.

- Work with students in a youth group or college ministry.

- Teach skills or hobbies to others, sharing your faith whenever possible.

- Go on organized summer missions projects.

- Attend Christian growth or ministry training seminars.

- Counsel other couples to center their relationships on Christ.

Building a Foundation

Make it your practice and determination to seek the Lord, to love Him fully, and to have a spiritual passion for Him whether dating or not dating. Develop personal spiritual characteristics that will provide a solid foundation for a future marriage relationship. Bring that passion for Christ into your friendships as you and another person seek the Lord and develop true spiritual harmony.

Ask God to bring about togetherness through internal motivation. Don't try to force another person to love you.

Look for open spaces in a relationship where you can grow and build spiritual oneness together. But be aware of obstacles. Discern through prayer, interaction with each other, and the Scriptures whether these obstacles are opportunities for growth together or fences put up by God to lead you apart.

Make dating an experience of spiritual growth. Whether the relationship ends up being a prelude to marriage or a preparation for developing other Star-balanced relationships, determine to become a friend by applying God's Word to your life with the power of the Holy Spirit.

Part Two

Hindrances to a Lasting Love

■ ■ ■

9

Shutting Off Transparency

■ ■ ■

From the time we are born, we want and need love. During World War II, in an overcrowded orphanage, physically healthy babies began to die for no apparent reason. Staff members paid close attention to providing for all their physical needs, but still they died. Finally, the staff realized that the children who lived were those who were cuddled and cared for by the overworked orphanage staff. No wonder those who go through life without experiencing intimacy and closeness with others have a difficult time.

Despite our desire and need for love, many people have a tendency to run from it. The closer you become to someone emotionally, the greater the potential for that person to reject or misunderstand you. We don't mind too much if a stranger shows a lack of interest in us, but if the ones we love most do not respond to us positively, we are devastated.

We want to overcome loneliness, enjoy intimacy, and experience deep friendship, but we don't want any pain to come with it.

My wife, Paula, and I love each other deeply, but we still manage to say and do things that hurt each other, even though we don't mean to. We've had to apologize to each other many times since we've been married. That's part of the reality of life. Painless love simply does not exist.

A friend of mine told me that by middle school, he had learned to protect his heart. He would give candy to a girl to show her that he liked her rather than say the words, "I like you." She might reject his words of affection, but she wasn't likely to reject the candy.

The desire to protect ourselves doesn't disappear after adolescence. Following one of my seminars on relationships, a woman in her 20s told me, "I'm taking steps never to be hurt again."

"Then, Whitney, you're taking steps never to love again," I warned her. "No matter what you do, you can't have love without experiencing some pain."

"Why not?" she said. "I want love, but I don't want to be hurt by another man again."

In one way or another, all of us have experienced some type of emotional trauma in our past relationships. Our hearts bear the scars and bruises of these battles. Consequently, we often develop defenses to protect ourselves from potential hurt and pain. These defensive roles, games, and masks become natural reflex actions for us. They not only hinder our ability to develop intimacy in our relationships with others but also stunt our personal growth.

Double Signals

We want intimacy, and yet we are afraid of potential emotional pain, so we give people a double signal. On one hand, we signal to them, "Come closer," while on the other hand we signal, "Stay away." We subtly communicate, "You're an attractive person, and I want to be needed and liked by you. I want closeness." At the same time, we shy away by hinting, "I don't want you to come too close because you may discover some of my vulnerable spots and reject me."

Walls of Protection

To protect our hearts, we build walls around them. We want to keep people from getting in to hurt us. But remember, the same wall that keeps people out also keeps us trapped inside by ourselves. When we build walls, we force ourselves to handle our problems and struggles alone—and that is loneliness. Being alone is not loneliness. A sense of facing life by yourself is loneliness.

We build these walls of protection over the years by avoiding emotional closeness with people, by steering conversation away from subjects or feelings that are potentially painful to us, and even by being offended when such subjects are broached.

Have you ever felt like there were two different people in your life? One is the outside person, the you everyone sees and talks to. We spend most of our time in this category. The other is the inside person that few people ever see. This is the deep-down-beneath-the-surface us. We are afraid to let this inside person be seen because we don't really like that part of us. It contains our weaknesses, real attitudes, and inadequacies—the dark side of our personalities. Yet, we desperately want people to love us for who we really are—to know and accept the inner us. We are afraid to open up the rusted gates to our hearts to let others in. So we hide for fear others will find out what we are really like and reject us. Instead of risking, we play it safe, hiding behind the emotional walls surrounding our hearts.

Robert Frost aptly said, "Do not build a wall until you know what you are walling in and what you are walling out."

Denial

Some people try to protect their hearts by denying that they really want or need someone else. Because of our society's emphases on self-sufficiency and independence, admitting we need each other is extremely difficult. It is considered a sign of weakness.

My own desire for a wife came in waves of emotions. Many times I went months without the least twinge of emptiness in my heart. My job took all my energy and creativity. Then something would snap. An old photograph, a love song on the radio, a glimpse of two lovers walking hand in hand, some fond memory of a former girlfriend, or a friend announcing his engagement would produce a huge wave of frustration with my singleness. I suddenly felt lonely and vulnerable. Only a wife could fill the void. I searched for the "right one for me," but there was no one I cared to give my heart to. I struggled to regain my composure and air of independence. Months of loneliness would alternate with months of self-sufficiency.

I finally decided to pray that God would take away my desire for a wife. I didn't know how to handle these undulating waves of desire. If only God would take away the deep loneliness or painful emotions I felt down inside. How could I admit openly to my friends that I really wanted a wife?

God, remove my attraction to women. Deaden my heart toward marriage.

One evening as I was in the middle of praying this prayer, I suddenly realized that God had created me with a desire for a wife. Why should I ask Him to obliterate it?

I'm grateful to God that He didn't answer those prayers. If He had answered them, I would not be married today. Instead, He gave me the strength to handle the waves of pressure and loneliness. As I faced and accepted my inner needs, He brought other friends and interests into my life to lessen my vacillation and to provide for my need to be loved. Eventually, He brought into my life the woman perfectly suited for me—in His time and in His way.

The Testing Game

Do you test other people and their feelings toward you in order to protect your sensitive heart? You may consciously study people's attitudes and responses to you—the way they look at you, how much they talk to you, or how they react to what you say or do. Based on your personal research, you may make a decision about how much of yourself you will reveal to them and how much you will interact emotionally with them. You always hold back until the other person passes your test. If two people both play this "cat-and-mouse" game, their relationship may never get started.

The Turtle Syndrome

To protect their hearts, some people become overly cautious and get caught up in what I call the turtle syndrome. Their head slowly extends out of their protective shell. They look around nervously, and if anything potentially dangerous is seen, their head quickly goes right back in again.

A woman may think, "If he calls me this week, then I'll know he cares. Otherwise, I am not going to be too friendly with him." A man may decide, "If she smiles and shows some interest when I talk with her, then I'll try to ask her out. But until I sense that, I am staying away."

Genuine vulnerability requires taking the initiative to communicate feelings without knowing if the other person will reciprocate. Dismantling the emotional walls that isolate you is worth the risk.

When we have been rejected and disappointed, we have a tendency to project that bad experience on all others of that sex. We are convinced that "they're all the same."

Quite often, a man won't ask a woman out because he thinks he might get turned down—rejected. He would rather sit at home all weekend than take that chance. If a woman would give him some subtle but definite encouragement, he might be more inclined to take the chance. But, of course, the woman doesn't want to be too obvious in showing her interest because the man may think she is too forward or pushy. She shows only the same polite interest that she might show any person, just in case he isn't interested. No one wants to look like a fool.

As a single person, I stayed at home many weekends because I didn't want to face the possibility of being turned down for a date. I thought, *If I don't ask, I can't be hurt.* But my timidity resulted in many lonely hours.

Busyness

To avoid exposing the inside person, some people retreat into a shell of busyness. They marry their work and become workaholics. They become totally involved in their jobs so that the distraction of being busy keeps them from facing their own needs or becoming involved in someone else's life. Avoidance is safer than vulnerability.

As a protection against getting too close to other people, a friend of mine got so involved in his work that eventually he had a nervous breakdown. As head of a large organization, he had little time for anyone or anything else. After a while, he began to have all kinds of pain and physical ailments that led to the breakdown. Hiding from others or from ourselves without negative consequences is impossible.

Finally, if we do arrange a date, we still act like emotional turtles by sticking only to small talk. We bottle up our feelings, fears, dreams, and sorrows and end up with superficial relationships. As a result, we relate only to others' outside person—how they look, act, or dress. We remain attracted only for superficial reasons because that's all we want to know of that person.

No wonder a typical date includes getting something to eat, going to a movie or club, and then making out. It has no risk, no sharing, no real communication, no true companionship.

The person experienced in this type of superficial behavior has a hard time interacting with someone on a deeper level. The habit of hiding in a shell is a difficult one to break.

Giving in the Wrong Way

Some people protect their hearts by letting sex communicate for them. They give their bodies to people but never give their inner selves—their minds and hearts. The inside person is well hidden.

People also protect their hearts by giving things instead of themselves. They readily give material gifts but never give of themselves emotionally. It's too frightening to be so vulnerable.

Some parents do this with their children. A number of my friends have told me that their parents never sat down with them to find out what they were really like deep inside. Nor would their parents readily share about themselves. These friends had to judge their parents' love by the material things they were given, a poor substitute for true, intimate love.

The Cover-Up

Other people hide behind their strengths or positive personality traits to avoid expressing their weaknesses and vulnerabilities. So what's wrong with that? After all, shouldn't you put your best foot forward? But if you only put your best foot forward, your weak foot never has a chance to become stronger. Other people see you as a superficial person.

Sarah enjoys asking questions and finding out about other people. Asking puts her in control of conversations. Although people like Sarah's attention, they never find out anything about her. She is always playing the part of the counselor without revealing what is going on inside her own life and heart.

Tom is a comedian, the life of the party. He uses his strength—jokes and laughter—to keep people at arm's length. In this way, he avoids letting others know what's really going on inside of him. Many famous comedians are people who are or have been desperately lonely and fearful of others.

Lynn hides behind knowledge. She has a ready answer for everything, for any situation. She wants to be helpful, so giving advice about every problem is a priority to her. However, Lynn doesn't allow a hurting person to feel any pain or grief. She is too quick to offer them a myriad of answers instead of being sensitive to what they are feeling.

Surely, we must try to handle or overcome our problems. But when hurting people try to change immediately from sorrow to joy without dealing adequately with the underlying causes, they may find themselves with deeper emotional troubles later on. A hurting person needs someone who can comfort and empathize so that the hurt and sorrow can come out and not be denied. As Romans 12:15 says, "Weep with those who weep."

Lynn has a hard time allowing other people to express their emotions and pain because she can't face her own hurts and sorrows. She denies the reality that people need to feel suffering because she doesn't want to face her own struggles. Lynn fears that if she faces her own problems and can't overcome them, her strength—her knowledge, which she assumes is wisdom—would be undermined. But knowledge requires experience to grow into wisdom. Lynn refuses to *experience* the ups and downs of life. If she did, she would have more wisdom in dealing with people. Others may admire her positive answers for every situation, but they know her only as an opinionated person, one who faces life with her mind but not with her emotions.

Fear and Intimacy

Let's look at the fears that cause us to shut off vulnerability and honesty.

1. The Fear of Rejection

Have you ever let someone see beneath the surface and get to know your inside person? What a scary and vulnerable position that can be! If we share who we really are, we have nowhere to hide.

If people we have loved hurt us, we fear that history will repeat itself and that we might find ourselves devastated again. We may be tempted to say, "I have learned my lesson; I will never again entrust my heart to someone who has the potential to hurt me deeply." But we make a crippling mistake when we cut ourselves off from the relationships that God wants to bring into our lives, even if those involve some hurt along the way.

2. The Fear of Losing Control

Some men may fear losing control of their independence in a relationship that might limit their freedom. On the other hand, some women may fear having their identities submerged in a relationship with a man.

3. The Fear of Facing One's Loveless Life

A Christian psychotherapist in Dallas told me that some people approaching the possibility of real love and intimacy will refuse it because they have never known it before. Subconsciously, they realize that if they experience genuine closeness now, they face the reality that they haven't experienced it before. They are likely to think, *If I let you get close to me, I may be overwhelmed with the realization that I've never been loved this way before. I don't know how to respond, and my empty heart may spoil everything.*

One shudders to think that his or her whole life has been lived bankrupt of real love. The person runs from love instead of recognizing his or her emptiness and responding to love.

Destructive Fear

Fear causes us to be self-protecting; love is self-giving. Fear causes us to be preoccupied with ourselves. Our fears, loneliness, and emotional pain become the focus of our attention. We cannot be self-giving because we turn inward and are busy protecting ourselves.

Fear also destroys our ability to fully receive the love that others show us. Self-centeredness and self-absorption isolate us from others and deepen our loneliness and pain.

I saw this when I was in college, involved in a ministry to people on skid row in Chicago. Each Sunday afternoon a group of us guys would travel to an area of the city famous for its sleazy hotels and derelicts. Just about every week, I met a homeless man named Sam. We discussed lots of issues in his life, including his relationship with God. I was amazed that he knew the Bible better than I did! If I started to quote a verse to him, he would finish quoting it. Yet he refused to open his life to God or to trust God to change his life. He didn't want God to control what he was used to controlling—his miserable, failed life. Sam was afraid to open up and receive love from anyone else. He couldn't see that protecting his sensitive heart and trusting no one actually made him all the more isolated and vulnerable to the onslaughts of life. He was his own prisoner.

We may not go to the same extent of isolation. But too many of us react as Sam did. We try to achieve safety and happiness by protecting ourselves. Eventually, self-absorption leads to a life that is no bigger than ourselves, and that, my friend, is true misery.

Breaking Down the Wall

What can we do to break down the wall of protection we have built around our hearts? Here are six actions that will help us out of our isolation.

1. Accept God's Acceptance of You

God's love for you is unconditional. Realize that you are secure in Him. You can be confident that He is never going to leave you nor forsake you (Hebrews 13:5), regardless of what you are facing. He understands you. He didn't make a mistake when He created you (Psalm 139). When you came along, He didn't sneeze. He wasn't on vacation. He didn't say, "Oops, I didn't do a good job on that one!" You may not like some things about yourself, but God does not in any way reject you if you have put your faith in Him (Romans 5:8; 1 John 4:18).

2. Look at Christ's Example of Vulnerability

Jesus was criticized, maligned, and rejected. Everyone eventually abandoned Him to His hateful accusers, but still He was willing to open Himself to people. He sat down with His followers and instructed them to live godly lives in a perverse world. He fielded the barbed questions of His enemies with wisdom and kindness. He didn't try to isolate Himself and protect His heart. Jesus was not fearful of being hurt even by those He loved because He knew how completely His Father loved Him; He was secure in that love. No matter who rejected Him, He felt safe in His Father's love and acceptance.

That same fulfilling love that Jesus knew can sustain us as well. The night before Jesus was betrayed by Judas and nailed to the cross, He prayed to His Father that the world might know that "you sent me and have loved them [all believers] as you have loved me" and that "the love even you have for me may be in them."[1] As we come to realize that love, the fear of rejection and even rejection itself will not devastate us.

3. Deal with the Fears and Hurts

Be brutally honest with yourself. Do you have difficulties relating to someone in significant and deep issues? What are you afraid of? Ask the Lord to help you overcome these fears. Some emotional scars may take a long time to heal, but the Lord wants you to move ahead with His courage in spite of those wounds. In that way the fears will decrease. Dealing with your failures and hurts from the past helps to release you from your present fears.

4. Share Your Life with Others

Begin to open up and share the inside you, including your failures and growth. The more secure you become in God's love and acceptance, the more you can risk rejection. Reveal yourself to others first; then they will feel comfortable enough to reveal themselves to you. As they see you accept yourself as an imperfect person on the road to maturity, they will realize that you are free to accept their imperfections as well. Mutual openness will deepen your undertanding of each other and draw you closer together.

When I was 34, I started a small fellowship group with nine other men. Our CELL group—Christians Encouraging, Learning, and Loving—met in my office for two hours every Tuesday night to talk about our needs, read the Bible, and pray for each other. We went on camping trips and played basketball together. With them I could be myself and reveal who I really was and where I was in my life and Christian growth. We learned not only about each other but about ourselves. We became intimate friends for life.

As the men in my CELL group became involved in each other's lives, we began to reach out to help people outside our group as well. Jesus gave a foundational principle of life, "It is more blessed to give than to receive."[2]

5. Let Others Help You

I find a lot of people who are willing to give help but are not willing to receive it. They are always the first to lend a helping hand in time of need, but they refuse to be helped. I know a woman who is always giving her time and money to help people, but she has a hard time accepting anything she is offered. This one-sided generosity is actually a subtle form of pride. Often such people feel responsible for others but cannot admit that they themselves have needs that others can meet. They are emotional one-way streets. On the other hand, some people have a selfish outlook on life, wanting others to always listen to their hurts. They take but rarely give help. Such people are usually ignorant of how much they exhaust the strength of others.

As we continue to change habits that hinder good relationships, the walls around our hearts will start to collapse. Then we will begin to become whole people, able to give and receive love deeply. We will become emotional two-way streets.

10

Pressing for Instant Intimacy

■ ■ ▪

When I lived in Bloomington, Indiana, I became so irritated at having to wait at traffic lights that I checked the amount of time different lights throughout the city stayed red. I avoided the longer ones. To my surprise, I discovered that the average light stayed red all of 45 seconds! You would have thought it was close to 45 minutes if you knew how often I became impatient waiting for a green light.

Many people have had similar feelings. We don't like to wait when the traffic light is red or get stuck in traffic behind a slow-moving vehicle. Looking at all the irritated drivers makes me think we consider ourselves kings or queens of the road. Every light should be green for us, and everyone should get out of our way. "Wait" is a word we don't like to hear, let alone experience. A "me first" attitude reigns supreme.

We're members of the instant gratification generation, a group that expects immediate fulfillment of our every desire. We click some computer keys, and our monitor screen displays information that once took hours or days to find in libraries or stacks of records. We buy fast machines only to become dissatisfied with them because in a few months they are obsolete when even faster machines come on the market.

We have e-mail, cell phones, personal shoppers—anything to cut the time and work necessary to meet our needs and wants. If we have to wait three minutes for a hamburger at McDonald's, we consider the service slow. We have disposable everything—from diapers to eating utensils, from drink cans to razors—all designed to increase the pace of our lives. We use and toss, use and toss. We get irritated if anything slows us down. We are impatient people.

In the same way, many of us want the building of relationships to be quick, exciting, and without hindrances. We want to feel good now, and we don't want to think about the consequences. We want intimacy, fun, and thrills but no commitment. We go to the bars, to the gym, and to singles groups to pick up someone or to be picked up.

When it's over, we know that we touched someone's body but never touched their soul.

The instant gratification generation chooses the immediate, superficial fulfillment of our needs, rather than waiting for better, more permanent solutions in the future. We have difficulty putting off momentary pleasure for lasting satisfaction. True intimacy takes time. It takes vulnerability. It takes commitment and faithfulness. It takes sacrifice and trust. But these qualities are not valued or easily developed in our society.

Though sex involves all of who you are, it doesn't require love. Unfortunately, the terms "sex" and "love" are often used interchangeably. When we confuse these two, we may momentarily satisfy our passions, but we ultimately end up with an empty heart. We want genuine love and oneness, but often we settle for a superficial sexual experience. The result is disillusionment. What we really desire is not sex; we want an enjoyable and lasting intimacy. But how can that be obtained?

Remember the Relationship Star

Remember the Star's five important areas of our lives—the physical, emotional, mental, social, and spiritual. By God's design, happiness and fulfillment are results of balance in these areas. When they are out of balance, we experience frustration, emptiness, and sometimes, a burned-out feeling.

When we try to develop a special relationship with a person of the opposite sex, we often look for an instant solution. Where do we find it? Usually, it's in the physical area. It's easier to become physically intimate with someone than to be intimate in any of the other four areas. You can become physically intimate in an hour or less. It just depends upon the urge! But eventually you discover that this provides only momentary relief for a much deeper need. In fact, physical intimacy without marriage commitment is not intimacy at all. It's a barrier to true intimacy.

Gina was dating Ryan. The more they got to know each other, especially in his apartment, the more they realized they wanted each other physically. One night they had sex, which at first was thrilling but later produced tremendous frustration in Gina's heart. She had exposed her body but had not received what she wanted—true closeness and mutual commitment with the one she thought she loved. Their relationship eventually ended in guilt and disappointment.

As we saw earlier, the more a couple gets involved physically, the less they communicate about significant topics. Their conversations become shallow. Too often, physical involvement merely means that two self-centered people are seeking satisfaction for self-centered desires. Genuine love and total life-sharing are missing. Premarital sexual involvement is a shortcut to love, but the detour ends at a dead end. We defeat the very reason we want true intimacy, which is to find lifelong companionship and satisfaction.

The Law of Diminishing Returns

At the bottom of all this is the law of diminishing returns. Concerning unmarried couples and their sexual involvement, this principle states that the more you do it, the less satisfying it is.

The following graph illustrates this. The vertical line represents the level of excitement in a relationship, the horizontal line the amount of time the relationship has been in effect. When a relationship is new, the graph line goes up sharply when the man first embraces the woman and they exchange kisses. It's an exciting new adventure with one another and the romantic feelings are thrilling.

**Level
of
Excitement**

Kissing

Petting

Intercourse

Time

After a while, the hugs and kisses become a habit and the level of excitement drops. The graph line peaks and then begins to go down. In order to raise the level of excitement, the couple will begin to make out or experiment with touching each other's bodies. Again, the thrill increases and the excitement escalates.

For the moment, they feel exhilarated by the rush of passion and the warm closeness that follows. Eventually, that too is unable to satisfy and becomes frustrating.

Each person begins to feel unfulfilled. Both realize that their relationship is incomplete. The temptation to go further, to do more, to go all the way seems overwhelming. Why deprive ourselves? Eventually, the couple is likely to culminate their passion by having sex. They climb to the heights of pleasure only to discover unexpectedly that they are still empty. Dissatisfaction, guilt, disappointment, and disillusionment result, and the level of excitement goes down, down, down into the negative zone. The thrill is fleeting and frustration increases.

From all we hear today, sexual intercourse should be the apex, the greatest experience of life. The vast majority of sexual scenes in movies and popular books are between a man and a woman who are not married to each other. Sex without the commitment of marriage is trumpeted as the usual behavior of couples.

However, reality is far from the Hollywood bed scene. Sex outside marriage in the real world points to a very different outcome, one in which people who are physically involved before marriage face devastating results. Sex can bring an unmarried couple thrills. But without true intimacy, the thrills wear off quickly. Soon they feel used and empty, and they eventually argue and break off the relationship.

What a way to end a promising relationship! It starts with excitement and hope, but it ends with bitterness. In fact, sexual burnout may be the primary reason why dating relationships are destroyed. A couple gets too close too soon.

The Morning-After Syndrome

This pattern is what I call the "morning-after syndrome." A sexually active couple awakes to find that intimacy is fleeting. After a night of passion, they wake up to a living nightmare. They may not even want to talk or to look at each other. They just want to escape. The sexual relationship doesn't satisfy them anymore, and what they end up with is not what they really wanted. Realizing that genuine love and intimacy cannot be obtained instantly, they find themselves still searching for genuine fulfillment.

No matter what our friends and the media tell us, the driving desire of each human being is not for sex or romance; it is for true intimacy.

Sexual activity can be very deceptive because it gives a feeling of intimacy, but it is a facade. You are tricked into thinking more intimacy exists than really does. Physical intimacy does not mean that a couple is intimate in the other areas of their lives. We fall in love with love and passion rather than with the person as he or she really is. Sexual involvement without a marriage commitment focuses on techniques of sexual performance and turning each other on. Rushing to instant self-gratification, we miss total-person intimacy. We rob each other of true joy and pleasure.

Sex Is God's Idea

Because God created us with our emotional and sexual makeup, He is the expert on the subject of sex. He's the one who thought up the whole idea in the first place. When God speaks on the subject of sex, He gives the best principles to live by. These are not designed to spoil our fun but to give us total-person intimacy. God always wants to protect us from harm and provide us with the most satisfying and fulfilling sex life.

It was not modern psychology that discovered the problems involved with sex outside of true love and total commitment in marriage. The Bible warned us of that thousands of years ago. When God created sex, He knew that the physical feelings involved would drive us toward it. He wanted it that way, among other reasons, in order to continue the human race.

Sex and Procreation

God gave us commandments to keep sex within marriage so that the love of two people could produce another life that could grow up in the secure, loving, and nurturing environment of a family. Such an environment is crucial for the development of healthy personalities. Procreation within a family environment is a major reason not only for the sex drive but also for keeping it within marriage. However, it is not the only reason for God's commandments against adultery and fornication.

In the past, avoiding an unwanted pregnancy was the main reason "responsible" people waited until marriage to consummate the sexual act. Once contraceptives and legal abortions became available, that reason for abstaining from sex outside marriage became much weaker. Pregnancy was still a risk, but far less so. No longer did the fear of pregnancy keep two people who were romantically attracted to one another from considering sex as just an enjoyable pastime. Other significant reasons for keeping sexual relations within marriage could be ignored as long as the physical risk and resulting social risk acted as deterrents.

Sex and Intimate Union

God created our physical bodies, our ability to have sexual relations, and the physical feelings sex produces. He also created the romantic emotions and our desire for openness and commitment to one person for a lifetime.

Another reason, then, for keeping sex within marriage is that God designed it to produce an intimate union between a man and woman totally committed to each other. Genesis 2:24-25 says: "For this reason a man shall leave his father and his mother, and be joined to his wife; and they shall become one flesh. And the man and his wife were both naked and were not ashamed."

"They shall become one flesh" is not only physical oneness but also an emotional, intellectual, social, and spiritual bonding that sex provides. Only a small part of intercourse is physical. Sex was never intended by God to be merely a physical experience. He created sex to have emotional effects, even on a subconscious level. Sexual intercourse is a whole-person act, so it is both the culmination and expression of the deep intimacy that has been and will continue to be developed between a couple committed to spending the rest of their lives together.

The Old Testament word for sexual intercourse is "to know." To have sex, in biblical terms, is to know your spouse intimately. The implication is that sex involves not only a physical nakedness but a total nakedness—knowing the person on all levels, openly and vulnerably.

Within marriage, we are free to give ourselves completely and unreservedly, feeling "naked and unashamed" before our spouse. Because of the lifetime commitment, a complete love-trust relationship can be developed without the fear of being judged as unacceptable by our spouse. The marriage commitment includes lifetime acceptability, so we need not fear desertion and rejection.

To have sex is to give intimate knowledge of yourself away. God wants to protect us from losing part of ourselves to someone who will not be with us for a lifetime. Once you have given that knowledge of yourself away, you can never get it back. When the person to whom you have given yourself walks out of your life, part of you goes, too.

When I was in graduate studies at Indiana University, I was required to attend a human sexuality conference at which a psychologist spoke. The group included doctors, nurses, professors, and other graduate students. During one afternoon session, the psychologist spoke of virginity. She told a lot of jokes, and everyone got a big laugh. She was putting virginity down and making fun of it. I didn't laugh. I'd bet a billion dollars God didn't laugh, either. Do you know why? God has designed sex to be beautiful and pure within His guidelines of marital commitment. Virginity is the only thing in our lives that we can give to one person one time only. It's the most precious physical and emotional gift we can give to anyone.

God's purpose is for us to give our virginity to the one person with whom He has united us in marriage. It is the unique seal of commitment to love and cherish our spouses all our lives.

In sex we expose ourselves in the most vulnerable way possible. Our innermost being is unprotected as at no other time. Within marriage, this can cause a deepening of the relationship and growth of the two people. Outside the protective shelter of marriage, we open ourselves to the deepest heartaches possible. God wants to protect our hearts, our minds, and our innermost beings.

Sex and Pleasure

A third purpose for which God created sex was to increase the pleasure of marriage. God designed sex to produce and enhance relational intimacy, and pleasure is a by-product.

God knows that real sexual enjoyment and fulfillment come when we experience total freedom in a relationship. If we are unable to experience emotional and physical freedom, we will also miss out on the enjoyment. The marriage relationship brings total sexual freedom because only in a total, lifetime commitment is freedom possible on all levels of life—emotional, mental, social, spiritual, and physical. Marriage produces safety and security. A person can therefore give unreservedly to his or her spouse without fear of rejection.

Sex in marriage is also free of guilt. You can know that God smiles on and is pleased with your sexual relationship. God never intended us to be ashamed of our bodies, of sexual touching, or of anything related to the sexual relationship between a husband and wife. We can let go of inhibitions and totally enjoy each other.

True sexual enjoyment comes only with emotional freedom stimulated by lifetime commitment and the absence of guilt. Yet along with this, a deep friendship with communication and transparency must be present. When we are able to be ourselves and be emotionally "naked" without fear, we are free to give ourselves to the relationship. The ability to give ourselves freely, completely, and unreservedly on all levels is crucial to experiencing the joy and pleasure God intended sex to bring to a husband and wife.

When we have sex outside the boundaries that God has set up for our protection and provision, we end up cheating ourselves. God is more concerned about our happiness, our relationships, and our sexual fulfillment than we are. He wants the very best for us, not only today but also in the future. He doesn't want us to lack any good thing. This is why God has clearly said no to sex outside the protective walls of marriage.

Three Kinds of Love

What is love? Songs have been sung about it. Poets have written about it. Movies have tried to portray it. Best-selling books have described it. But it still remains elusive. By looking at the divorce statistics and the number of unhappy homes, we can see that few marriage relationships achieve it.

In Greek, the original language of the New Testament, three different words are translated "love" in English. One is the word *eros*. It is a very self-centered, sexual love. Bluntly stated, *eros* has this attitude: "I like me, you like me; we now both like the same person!" The second word for "love" is *phileo*. It is a brotherly love, back and forth, between two people—good friends. "I like you, you like me." The third word is *agape*. This is a total, selfless, giving love that does not demand or require a response from the other person. "I love you regardless of your feelings about me."

The way we usually love is to start with *eros*. We see someone who turns us on romantically. We want to get involved with him or her in order to meet our own needs. We may eventually grow into the *phileo* stage of love with that person. But we rarely get to the *agape* stage because we are self-centered and insecure, and we want to protect our hearts.

The only person who has ever exhibited pure *agape* love—giving total love before receiving anything in return—is God. In fact, God always starts with *agape* love. He says,

> This is love *[agape]*: not that we loved *[agape]* God, but that he loved *[agape]* us and sent his Son as an atoning sacrifice for our sins. Dear friends, since God so loved *[agape]* us, we also ought to love *[agape]* one another. No one has ever seen God; but if we love *[agape]* one another, God lives in us and his love *[agape]* is made complete in us."[1]

Three-Person Intimacy

To bring God into a relationship seems foreign to all that our culture tells us, yet I believe that real intimacy with another person can be found only when we have, first of all, true *agape* intimacy with the Creator.

God knows all about each of us. He knows about and understands every detail. God wants us to have intimacy with Him as well as with others. As the creator of sex, He has revealed the best plan for us to get the greatest fulfillment from it. God is not out to make us miserable. He loves us and wants us to be happy. Our society has distorted God's design for love, sex, and intimacy into superficial emotions and feelings. Love is more than emotions, and it is much more than a good feeling. The love God wants us to have is exciting, fulfilling, and lasting. But it can be obtained only by first having a personal relationship with Him.

But how does this work? How does having a personal relationship with God affect intimacy with others, particularly with those of the opposite sex?

The Nature of God's Love

To understand God's perspective of love, we must reject what our society tells us about love and intimacy, and adopt a new frame of mind. Since the beginning, God has tried to tell people that He loves them. But when the God of the universe, the Creator of us all, says "I love *(agape)* you," what does that include? Here are four elements of God's love for us.

God's Love Is Eternal.

He tells us through the ancient prophet Jeremiah, "I have loved you with an everlasting love."[2] God's love is never going to leave us, and that's exciting.

God's Love Is Kind.

The Hebrew word that we translate "loving-kindness" is used 180 times throughout the Old Testament to show God's attitude of love and kindness toward people. If God were out to make us miserable, do you think He would continually tell of His loving-kindness—180 times?

God's Love Is Forgiving.

Each of us is self-centered and rebellious, living the way we want to live. This is what the Bible calls sin. Our sin separates us from God and His love. In this condition, God considers us enemies[3] and destined for hell.[4] But the Bible tells us, "If we confess our sins, He is faithful and righteous to forgive us our sins and to cleanse us from all unrighteousness."[5] God not only forgives the sins we confess to Him but also forgets them and erases their penalty. As a result, God gives us salvation from hell. Eternal life—God's life in us, both on this earth and in heaven—is now our personal possession.

God's Love Is Giving.

God loved us so much that He sent Jesus Christ to die on the cross for our sins so that we might receive God's gift of eternal life. A very familiar Bible verse says, "For God so loved the world, that He gave His only begotten Son, that whoever believes in Him shall not perish, but have eternal life."[6] Giving Jesus Christ over to death in order to provide the way for us to live eternally with Him showed how great God's love is for us. All of God's promises come true for you when you "believe in Him"—when you put your trust in Christ as the only way to receive salvation.

Experiencing God's Love

God's love is totally different from what society defines as love. We can experience *agape* love when we come into a personal relationship with Christ. The Bible tells us that forgiveness and eternal life are ours simply by putting our faith in Him.[7] If we refuse to trust Christ, we cut ourselves off from receiving forgiveness and eternal life.

Once you trust Him for His love and forgiveness, you will begin to experience a personal relationship and growing intimacy with Him that lasts not only a lifetime but also for eternity. This relationship starts when you put your faith in Christ. Here is a sample prayer that you might want to pray:

> Lord Jesus, I know I am a self-centered person and that I need You. You are God, and You gave Your life on the cross for my sins. I ask You to forgive me of my self-centeredness and sin. I put my faith and trust in You and receive You into my life. I ask You to make me the kind of person You want me to be. Thank You for forgiving me and giving me eternal life as You have promised.

Whether you have just made this commitment to God or did it a long time ago, you need to understand what type of love God has for you. You may think His love for you is conditional, dependent on your feelings of closeness to Him. No matter how you feel, His *agape* love for you is always unconditional. If you sin, confess those sins to Him, and He will forgive. However, if you refuse to obey Him, He will discipline you as a father disciplines a child.[8] Remember, His love for you does not diminish with time or circumstance.

When you realize this, you will know that you are totally loved. You don't need to reach out desperately to others to receive love. You have unconditional *agape* love from God, full and flowing over, enough to give to others, whether or not you receive love from them. You will realize that love and intimacy are much more than what you have experienced before. Love and intimacy involve the whole of life and, when including the sexual area, are meant to be experienced through a lifelong marriage commitment and trust.

Saying Yes and Being Sorry

E rnest Hemingway once said, "What is moral is what you feel good after and what is immoral is what you feel bad after."

The question remains, How long after? Sometimes the most devastating consequences of premarital sex don't show up until some time has passed. Unfortunately, many people find that the long-range consequences of sex outside of marriage produce problems that far outweigh the temporary ecstasy they felt during the sexual experience.

God commanded us to limit sexual intercourse to marriage because He loves us and wants only the best for us. He knows the attraction of sex. He created it.

Within God's protective boundaries of marriage, sex can be a warm expression of a couple's lifelong commitment to one another, further bonding their cohesiveness and oneness. It will culminate, on the physical level, in a union that is already developing on all other levels.

Sex outside of marriage eventually brings regret. A person may not always trace the pain and consequences to its source—a misuse of God's gift of sex. God gave us many warnings against adultery and fornication, not to limit our happiness but to maximize it. Those who do not understand or refuse to believe God's warnings often find that premarital sex can turn into a monster.

In all my years of counseling individuals and speaking at conferences for singles and married couples, I have never heard anybody say they were sorry that they waited until marriage to give themselves sexually to their spouse. But I have heard hundreds say they were sorry that they didn't wait.

A Dangerous Lie

That is not what you would expect to hear after listening to the words of popular songs or seeing the visual messages in the movies, TV, and print media. They all elevate sex outside marriage as the greatest and best. "Get what you want now." They never portray the consequences. Beer commercials show lots of good-looking people having a party drinking alcohol. They never show the devastation alcoholism brings to individuals and families. Do you think they would sell many cans of beer if the commercial showed real drunken derelicts on skid row or a three-car accident where several people were killed because a driver was drunk?

Love stories in the movies don't include scenes from the life of an AIDS patient or the horror of doctors aborting an unwanted baby. Pornography websites don't show you the awful trauma and devastated lives of rape victims. Sensual magazines and fantasy novels don't write about sexual liaisons that produce hateful divorce battles or the seared lives of children who are victims of destroyed marriages.

Sexual promiscuity produces hollow promises, devastated dreams, violence, shattered marriages, and scarred children. Sex without marital commitment is shallow and unfulfilling. It leaves countless broken lives in its path. People are blindsided by the devastating results of the misuse of sex. They extol the pleasures of ending a date in bed and advocate premarital sex as a way to satisfy all their passions and bring unparalleled happiness. All the while, they refuse to recognize the longer-lasting consequences that may occur to themselves and to those with whom they are involved.

This is not an easy chapter to write and probably not an easy chapter to read. But you will never fully appreciate the wonder of godly love until you consider the consequences of fleshly lust. Sex outside marriage brings many painful, long-range results. The old saying "Sow the wind and reap the whirlwind" describes our situation. We are drinking the dregs of our sex-crazed society.

Hope for Fulfillment and Restoration

On a personal level, God loves you and offers the best plan for satisfaction of your deepest longings and desires. He is not trying to make you miserable. God has provided the very best way for you to satisfy your desires for intimate companionship and marital oneness. But the Lord also wants to protect you from the misuse of sex.

After reading about these consequences, singles who have committed sexual sins may wonder if they have any hope for a fulfilling life and marriage in the future. Yes, they do! If there were no restoration of purity, I would never write this book. If God could not provide any means of healing, then I would not have any reason to continue my ministry.

Here is the great news. God offers you renewal—rejuvenated relationship with Him, energizing power of the Holy Spirit, and satisfying relationships based on biblical values. Although the road to healing may include tests and trials, you can have hope for peace, happiness, and fulfillment.

Negative Consequences

First, we need to reflect on the consequences of sex outside marriage. You probably won't find this information in the popular media or from people who advocate sexual permissiveness. If you jump off the roof of a tall building, you will quickly encounter the law of gravity. When you land on the ground below, it probably will be very painful. You break the law and the law will break you. When you break God's moral law, it will break you. Sexual involvement outside marriage leads to inevitable consequences.

I mention just a few of the repercussions not to scare you but to make you aware of the potential dangers of premarital sex. Just because a person says that he loves you does not mean that he will be faithful to you. You have no idea of his sexual history. If he will go to bed with you without being married to you, he probably has done the same thing with someone else before you. If he does not love you enough to reserve himself sexually for you until you are married, you are probably not the last person he will have sex with.

An empty "I love you" is not worth a lifetime of regret and physical pain. God wants to protect you from these devastating results.

Psychological Consequences

When I have lectured on developing quality relationships with the opposite sex, I've noticed that facts and statistics about the physical and social consequences of sex outside marriage usually don't bother some people who are sexually active. The facts don't seem to motivate them to change their behavior. They want to continue to have sex with people regardless of how it might affect them. The desire for sex overcomes any thoughts that they may contract a sexually transmitted disease (STD). They hope that using a condom will prevent disease or a potential pregnancy. If that doesn't work, drugs will relieve the disease, and an abortion will solve an unwanted pregnancy.

However, when I mention the negative psychological or relational consequences, those same people often take notice. These results of sex outside marriage have no easy solutions.

1. Guilt

When you violate your conscience or break God's moral law, guilt floods your mind and heart. It is an intellectual and emotional response to wrong actions and attitudes. The guilt is both psychological and spiritual.

Sometimes, counselors find wounds that have been covered up just as a scab covers a festering sore. The conscience can be numbed to the extent that there are no guilt feelings. Guilt has been submerged in a sea of rationalization and excuses—called guilt-desensitization. By indulging in something over and over, the conscience has been desensitized until it no longer bothers the person—at least not directly. Instead, the unresolved guilt comes out in other ways that seem unrelated to the original guilt-producing behavior. We become so familiar with what we are doing that the boundaries of right and wrong become blurred. Wrong no longer seems wrong.

Wayne told me about his own experience after I spoke to the singles group he attended. He found temporary pleasure from his first sexual experience. Afterward, he was overwhelmed by guilt and disgusted with himself. He knew that intercourse was meant for marriage. He was so upset by his actions that when he got home, he ran to the bathroom and vomited. Guilt flooded his emotions.

The next weekend, however, he and his girlfriend had sex again. This time, the experience was not followed by such extreme guilt reactions. Afterward, he felt miserable but didn't head for the bathroom. Eventually, after repeated sexual encounters, his guilt subsided completely. However, as time went on, a deeper repressed guilt and confusion about his whole life began tearing him apart.

Acknowledged or not, guilt is a destroyer. Repressed guilt can lead to depression, anger, rebellion, fear, anxiety, increasing inability to recognize one's own faults, and aggressiveness. Guilt also destroys relationships.

As a university student, Peter had been enthusiastic for the Lord. Although he was shy, Peter had summoned enough courage to ask Julie, who was also a Christian, for a date. This started a relationship that slowly became more physical. After graduation, they started sleeping together. Although both were Christians, their guilt was washed over by romantic passion. Peter moved into Julie's apartment. They lived together for three years, thinking their love was strong enough to handle any problems. But their arguments became more frequent as they tried to maintain separate identities.

Peter and Julie eventually separated with great anguish and hostility. The guilt and anger had driven him to violent behavior and stifling jealousy. He had threatened Julie and had followed her, watching her at a distance with binoculars. Julie belittled him constantly and angrily pierced his heart with her sharp tongue. They had left God out of their lives long ago. Now, Peter was depressed and refused to come back to God. The lingering guilt and frustration destroyed their relationship and drove them apart permanently.

2. Loss of Self-Esteem

Closely tied to guilt is the loss of self-esteem that results from going against both one's conscience and God's principles. This is due to a sense of shame. Self-esteem affects every area of people's lives, often governs their actions, and frequently impacts their relationships. Positive self-esteem is the basic element in any healthy person's personality. Loss of self-esteem can have a long-lasting and widespread effect on a person's life.

Michael enjoyed his relationship with Karen. He said he loved her and wanted to show that love more romantically. Although they were Christians, they allowed their relationship to become more physical. In the beginning, their sexual experience seemed right, and it was emotionally fulfilling for a long time. They continued to be involved in their Christian activities and felt only a small amount of hypocrisy. But eventually the dam burst, and feelings of guilt, shame, and immense self-disgust flooded their lives and relationship. Michael felt worthless; he wondered whether he would ever feel good about himself again. Slowly, his relationship with Karen disintegrated. They had glimpsed the depths possible in a sexual relationship, yet because it was outside the boundaries of marriage and God's purposes, the excitement they felt was only temporary. Eventually, their initial experience of love degenerated into a nightmare. Their lack of well-being became troublesome.

Michael eventually repented and asked God to forgive him for crossing the line with Karen. Even though he believed that the Lord forgave him for his sexual sins, it took several years for him to get over the shame. He hung on to verses in the Bible that assured him of God's grace and love for him. He once again began to see himself as clean in God's eyes.

Premarital sexual relations provide an easy way to use the other person to meet one's own physical desires. Many times the realization that you are not ultimately concerned for the other person's well-being produces feelings of self-disgust. This, in turn, causes a loss of self-esteem.

3. Flashbacks

Memories have a habit of exploding into the forefront of our minds at the most unlikely moments. Flashbacks of promiscuous sexual encounters can hinder a person from developing a new healthy relationship.

Flashbacks can be a sign of unresolved guilt about past activities. When guilt is suppressed, flashbacks may come back to your conscious mind as mental windows into your personal history. Often they are triggered by thoughts and circumstances that are similar to the old situation.

Jonathan, a close friend of mine, has been married for five years. He told me that he has been going through a difficult time in his relationship with his wife. Many times when they are making love, his mind is cluttered with thoughts of other women with whom he was once involved. These flashbacks have made it difficult for him to fully enjoy his wife.

How do you think his wife would feel if she knew he was thinking of other women when Jonathan was loving her? I don't think it would enhance their relationship.

4. Mental Pollution

From puberty on, we all experience sexual desires and fantasies. Added to this, the subject of sex dominates our society so much that it's hard to keep a pure mind as we go about our everyday lives. Entering a sexual relationship further increases the intensity of these lustful desires so that they become a powerful influence in our lives. The actual experience of sexual intercourse lasts but a short time compared to the amount of time a sexually active person thinks about and physically feels the desire for another sexual encounter.

Genuine love and sexual lust have many differences. Lust is never satisfied. When a person gives in to sexual temptation, his or her mind is even more preoccupied with sex. The heat has been turned up, and cooling down again takes a long time. You will grow weary of continually dealing with aroused and unfulfilled sexual desires when you would like to forget about the past. A dirty mind is tough to clean.

5. Sexual Inhibition

A somewhat opposite phenomenon has been named "inhibited sexual desire" or ISD by psychologists. The more well-known names for this are frigidity and impotence.

With greater promiscuity, sex becomes boring and unexciting. A person loses the thrill because illicit sex is so unsatisfying. The normal, natural enjoyment of sexual intercourse is robbed of pleasure and turns into a performance. To produce more excitement, a person delves into additional immoral sexual practices—pronography, bisexuality, multiple sex partners, bestiality, sadism, and mechanical devices.

Many people today are asking how to enjoy sex more. A plethora of articles are constantly being written to address this issue. The topic sells lots of books and magazines. But few give the biblical answer. If you follow God's plan and obey His commandments, sex in marriage is wonderful. Just read the Song of Solomon in the Bible.

Relational Consequences

1. Breakup

As I have already mentioned, sex tends to break up relationships because of guilt. But breakups also occur when the relationship is built on sexual attraction. This gives a false sense of intimacy, a mere illusion of what true intimacy really is.

Many singles have seen bad marriages (their parents') or have been stuck in bad relationships (their own marriages).

They want lasting love but not a lasting unhappy relationship. Some grew up in dysfunctional homes torn apart by bickering and fighting. Their parents fought fiercely through the dissolution of their marriage, and the kids were the battlefield. They were shoved around by the courts, lawyers, parents, step-parents, step-siblings, step-houses, step-schools, and step-friends. The thought of getting married and being imprisoned in a debilitating relationship makes them afraid of marriage. They do not want commitment—to anything, especially marriage. This is why over 5.3 million people are currently choosing to live with their boyfriend or girlfriend. They want the concept of marriage without the commitment.

However, cohabitation is a poor substitute for marriage. There's a good chance that an unmarried couple who lives together will never get married. Many experts estimate that approximately 50 percent of such couples will break off their arrangement. If the cohabitating couple does marry, they run a much higher risk of divorce.

Sex without commitment is merely convenient. It meets some needs in the man and woman but does not foster genuine oneness and mutual respect.

The seeds of divorce are planted long before marriage. Premarital sex is often a hidden but very real reason for divorce. The man and woman may say they love each other, but without commitment, they violate each other and lose respect. Their words are without integrity because each person is living a lie. Before marriage, sex may smother a couple's incompatibilities. In marriage, these irreconcilable differences, aggravated by a sense of mistrust, must be faced and may destroy the relationship.

2. Mistrust

How can you trust people who ask you to bare your body and soul but do not want to entrust their life to you?

Sex is not the superglue in a promiscuous relationship. It is an explosive. It will blow you apart with insecurity, anger, and fear. Without a lifetime commitment to one another, subtle but real insecurities and suspicions can eat a hole in your heart. Unsettling questions confront you. *Am I the only one? Will I be dropped for someone else? Will he (or she) stick around if I get sick?*

This lack of security may be carried over into marriage. If a person does not wait until after the wedding to have sex, there's no guarantee that signing the marriage license will change a person's character or habits. Promiscuous sexual habits do not die easily.

Mistrust also breeds possessiveness. With physical closeness comes emotional dependency. Like it or not, this is true, even in a casual affair. If you have made an emotional investment in someone you can't trust, you become more and more possessive. Afraid of losing your emotional investment, you try to control the person with whom you are involved. Giving him or her freedom is a fearful thing. Sex alone cannot guarantee he or she will be faithful to you. Sex alone is a very weak bond.

When I was a pastoral counselor, a couple on the brink of divorce came to see me. Steve was a well-to-do insurance man. Susan was his second wife. During Steve's previous marriage, he and Susan had become involved while she was his secretary. Moments of innocent flirtation in the office gradually led to a secretive affair. He divorced his first wife and married Susan.

When I saw them, Susan was staying at home, taking care of their child. But she kept remembering how Steve behaved in the office when she was his secretary. She could not trust him and he could not trust her. Susan feared that he might be involved with his present secretary or maybe some other female employee. She became more and more possessive and jealous. She constantly wondered where

Steve was and what he was doing. Their arguments mush-roomed. A deep root of bitterness and mistrust caused their marriage to deteriorate and eventually dissolve.

3. Comparison

People naturally tend to compare the present person they are involved with with former sexual partners. The more intimate and the more frequent sexual experiences one has had, the greater will be the tendency to analyze them. Sexual technique and performance become the center of attention in your lovemaking. You become more inter-ested in the techniques of being good in bed. Who got you the most excited? Who had the best body? Developing commitment and communication are not the main issues.

Comparison in any area of a relationship can under-mine it, but comparison in the physical area can devastate it. You focus on what you can get rather than on what you can give. When you feel disappointment in lovemaking, you will probably withdraw emotionally from the person. You may have a gnawing suspicion that the words "I love you" really mean "I love it (sex)."

Physical Consequences

The physical repercussions of sex outside marriage, such as contracting sexually transmitted diseases (STDs) and experiencing unwanted pregnancies, affect millions of people. Some people believe statistics always refer to other people, not to themselves. "I'm different," they say. "It won't happen to me." Yet, I have known hundreds who have been infected with STDs—always unexpectedly.

More than 65 million Americans are currently infected with an incurable STD. When you have sex with someone you do not know very well, you risk contracting a disease you will live with the rest of your life.

Here are just a few of the STDs that are prevalent today:

1. Herpes Simplex Virus (HSV)

Recently a teenager we know found out she has herpes. Her boyfriend gave it to her as they were "playing around." She will have it the rest of her life. Someday she will want to get married. How will she tell her perspective husband that she has this disease?

Over 45 million people in America are infected with genital herpes, one of today's most prevalent STDs. Infections are characterized by fever, swollen lymph nodes, and numerous clusters of painful vesicles on or near the genitals. These often develop into shallow ulcerations. They take weeks to heal but reoccur periodically. Drugs can lessen the symptoms of this disease, but it has no known cure.

2. Chlamydia

An estimated 3 million new cases of chlamydia are reported each year. That means 3 million people contracted this terrible disease from their sexual partners. What a miserable gift to give someone you "love."

Here is the surprising thing: 75 percent of infected women and 50 percent of infected men do not show symptoms. In other words, they don't know they are carrying the disease. So, when you ask them if they have an STD, they will say no. You will believe them and end up with the disease.

Chlamydia can severely damage the fallopian tubes in a woman and has now become one of the leading causes of infertility. Often women are unaware of the symptoms and may not find out they have it until years later when they discover they are infertile. In men, chlamydia causes an enlarged and tender prostate, inflammation of the urethra, and infection of the urinary tract. It is also responsible for conjunctival infection, respiratory tract colonization, and pneumonia in newborns and infants.

3. Gonorrhea

The prevalence of gonorrhea has increased dramatically in the last 20 years. Over 650,000 people get the disease each year. It affects the epididymis, prostate, and seminal vesicle in men. In some cases, it infects the pharynx. In women, it can cause urethral or vaginal discharge and frequently leads to inflammation of the fallopian tubes with subsequent damage and/or blockage. The problem is further complicated by the fact that 10 percent of all strains of gonorrhea are resistant to penicillin and other antibiotics.

4. Syphilis

Syphilis starts as a painless bump or chancre sore. But within weeks, the person develops symptoms such as headaches, sore throats, enlarged lymph nodes, joint aches and pain, weight loss, and a generalized skin rash. The infection then goes into the latent stage, without symptoms, that can later flare up and cause serious disease to the central nervous system or heart.

5. Pelvic Inflammatory Disease (PID)

Salpingitis, commonly called pelvic inflammatory disease, is an infection of the fallopian tubes and the surrounding areas or organs. It is usually, but not always, caused by gonorrhea or chlamydia. With this disease, a woman experiences severe abdominal pain, fever, and cervical discharge. Complications may include tubal abscess, infertility, and ectopic pregnancy. An abscess that ruptures into the body cavity is a surgical emergency, and death may quickly follow.

Every year, more than one million American women suffer an episode of PID, the most common complication of STDs. As many as 30,000 women annually undergo hysterectomies as a consequence of this disease. An estimated

100,000–150,000 women become infertile each year as a result of an STD that has resulted in PID.

6. Acquired Immune Deficiency Syndrome (AIDS)

At one time, AIDS in America was believed to be limited to the homosexual community and blood transfusion patients. Now it has spread to the heterosexual community.

Not only do people with the HIV virus who have symptoms pass on the disease, but so do carriers of the virus who have not yet developed any symptoms. An estimated 1 to 1.5 million people in America are infected with the HIV virus.

AIDS represents a wide range of clinical abnormalities, from severe infections and unusual cancerous processes to milder ones whose only symptoms are swollen glands, fever, and loss of weight. The virus has been found in the blood stream, the nervous system, and the brain. The AIDS-causing virus, HIV, destroys the immune system. No cure is presently available.

7. Genital Cancer

Cervical cancer, which kills more than 4500 American women each year, is strongly associated with several strains of Human Papilloma Virus (HPV), which infects 5.5 million people annually.

The risk of getting genital cancer increases with the number of sexual partners a woman has. Even if she becomes involved with only one man, her risk increases with the additional number of women with whom he has sexual relations.

8. Ectopic Pregnancies

Experts say that ectopic pregnancies (pregnancies that implant outside the uterus and most often in the fallopian tubes) have reached epidemic proportions.

Because STDs and PID can seal the fallopian tubes, the fertilized egg is prevented from lodging in the uterus. The resultant ectopic pregnancy causes serious complications. If it is not rectified soon, it can cause death.

9. Other Effects

Medical experts are now discovering that sexually transmitted diseases have a variety of other effects on the body. The list of problems includes tendonitis, arthritis, urethritis, hepatitis, abdominal pain, gastrointestinal infections, aseptic meningitis, and eye infections. STDs can affect almost any area of the body.

Obviously, premarital sex has the potential of causing great physical pain and misery, not just for a while but for a lifetime. I hope you do not take these ailments lightly. They can happen to you.

Condoms

The answer that is often given for the prevention of STDs is, Use a condom. Condoms are supposed to prevent the transmission of all sorts of diseases, including AIDS. While this barrier method does often work, it is certainly not totally effective. The media and concerned medical personnel will often employ the euphemism "Protect yourself" to mean "Use a condom." They used to call it "safe sex." Now they refer to it as "safer sex," silently acknowledging that there is no such thing as 100 percent safe sex.

The hype about condoms never mentions the ineffectiveness of the latex sheaths. Research has shown that their effectiveness in preventing STDs and AIDS is certainly not without questions. In order for a condom to prevent disease, it must be used correctly and not rupture—every time intercourse occurs. This is very difficult to achieve.

The Centers for Disease Control and Prevention (CDC) publishes reports on all kinds of medical and health issues. Their "Sexually Transmitted Diseases Treatment Guidelines" includes a report on condoms and their effectiveness.

> When used consistently and correctly, male latex condoms are effective in preventing the sexual transmission of HIV infection and can reduce the risk of other STDs (i.e., gonorrhea, chlamydia, and trichomonas). However, because condoms do not cover all exposed areas, they are likely to be more effective in preventing infections transmitted by fluids from mucosal surfaces (e.g., gonorrhea, chlamydia, trichomoniasis, and HIV) than in preventing those transmitted by skin-to-skin contact (e.g., herpes simplex virus [HSV], HPV, syphilis, and chancroid).[1]

The report goes on to say that the failure rate of condoms is 2 percent. That is, during 2 out of 100 episodes of intercourse the latex sheath breaks. Who knows when those two times will happen? One could break on the first incidence of intercourse.

At the end of the section on condoms, the report gives this warning: "Patients should be advised that condoms must be used consistently and correctly to be highly effective in preventing STDs."[2]

Translation: The condom has to be used correctly every single time, and even then it will fail 2 percent of the time.

However, a study reported in the Medical Institute for Sexual Health's advisory report entitled, "Condoms Are Probably Less Effective for Highly Contagious STDs" states: "The risk of infection by a highly infectious STD becomes quite high after multiple exposures, even in those who use condoms consistently."[3]

What does all this mean to you? Don't trust your life to a condom! A single night of sexual excitement may cause a lifetime of misery. Even worse, it may shorten your life. And even if the condom does protect against transmission of STDs and HIV, it cannot protect you against guilt, loss of self-esteem, flashbacks, mental pollution, sexual inhibition, breakups, or mistrust.

In the CDC's report on sexual transmission, the medical team of experts who presented the report gave the best way to fulfill your sexuality: "The most reliable way to avoid transmission of STDs is to abstain from sexual intercourse (i.e., oral, vaginal, or anal sex) or to be in a long-term, mutually monogamous relationship with an uninfected partner."[4]

Reserving yourself for marriage in order to consummate your marital vows with another person who has reserved him- or herself just for you is clearly the safest sex—and it is the most pleasurable. No disease. No emotional baggage. No regrets. Just the two of you loving each other the way God intended.

Social Consequences

When a man and a woman who are not married to each other start the process leading toward sexual involvement, they probably do not consider the long-term impact of their behavior. Most people don't want to hurt their sexual partner, themselves, or anyone else when they have sex. They just want to experience some pleasure and closeness with someone else. But a half-hour of sexual pleasure can bring a lifetime, even generations, of hurt and agony.

The social repercussions of sex outside marriage affect not only the couple but many others as well. Even the government (local, state, and national) and ultimately the taxpayers bear a huge burden providing public services to deal with social problems related to promiscuity.

1. Unwanted Pregnancies

We all know that there are no foolproof contraceptives. Despite their use, unwanted pregnancies do occur. The two people most affected are the woman and the child. Not only does a woman have an unwanted baby growing inside her, but the situation often causes tremendous social upheaval in her family. Family ties are severely strained as family members come to terms with what has happened.

But the most severe consequences are borne by the children. Twenty-eight percent of all babies born in America are from unwed mothers. In many cases the mother and/or father are unable or unwilling to financially take care of them. Many of these children are forced to live in foster homes. The stigma of their illegitimate birth can affect them their whole life.

2. Abortion

Each year in America, a million unwanted babies are aborted. The very people responsible for their existence—their mothers and fathers—decide to remove the "tissue" growing inside the womb. All the parents wanted was a little pleasure. But that fleeting pleasure turned into agonizing decisions, mental anguish, and emotional trauma. Some women carry tremendous guilt feelings the rest of their lives for their role in the murder of an unborn child.

3. Cultural Disintegration

A famous saying tells us, "The only thing we learn from history is that we don't learn from history." Time and again, the deterioration of a nation's moral fiber has led to its fall. A society begins to crumble from within when it is characterized by sexual permissiveness, a disintegration of the moral structure, and a failure to follow biblical concepts of morality. When choosing their sexual behavior, singles need to weigh not only personal considerations but also the effect their actions have on other people and society.

Spiritual Consequences

Of all the negative results of immoral sex, the spiritual consequences are the most severe. They eat away at the soul like a cancer and produce results that can last through all eternity. People may be concerned about the physical and relational aspects of their sexual actions because these hurt so much and create concern and worry. But they should have the same concern about the spiritual ramifications.

However, responses to spiritual consequences range from apathy to short-lived desires for change that produce tears with little genuine action. Such responses are further evidence of the devastating spiritual consequences of immoral sex.

1. Coldness Toward God

The word "sin" is used in the Bible to denote a deviation from the ways of God; it is the missing of the mark of God's righteousness, a transgression of God's law. In Romans 6:23 we are told, "The wages [results] of sin is death." "Death" here refers not only to eternal separation from God, as terrible as that is, but also to coldness toward God here and now. A person loses the excitement and joy of being a Christian.

The Bible becomes harder to read because it is a reminder of what that person's life should be. Prayer becomes less frequent unless a problem arises; then begging and pleading erupts from a hardened heart.

After his extramarital sex with Bathsheba, David hid from God for one year. In Psalm 32:3-4 he describes his agony: "When I kept silent about my sin, my body wasted away through my groaning all day long. For day and night [God's] hand was heavy upon me; my vitality was drained away as with the fever heat of summer." The person who hides from God is robbed of all the benefits of a close relationship with Him.

2. Coldness Toward Faithful Christians

When we walk in darkness, we don't want to be around people who walk in the light. They remind us of the joy that we no longer possess. Who wants to sing enthusiastically about a righteous God without righteousness inside the heart?

Some people, of course, get around this difficulty by going to Christian meetings, using Christian phrases, smiling at appropriate times during a Christian message, and singing Christian songs. But these people are empty of spiritual life. They have the appearance of Christianity, but they are dead inside. The Bible calls them hypocrites. They become critical of others who follow the Lord, but they have little personal interest in true dedication and faith. They simply put in their time while their hearts are like stone.

3. Misery

When one is running from God, misery eventually catches up. Then the person searches for someone to turn to.

That's what happened with Heather. She had heard me speak at a singles convention and wrote me a letter. Her story is a sad one.

> I met Jesus Christ when I was 12 years old. My spiritual life had several ups and downs, but now I'm in the deepest down. I don't remember my last faithful prayer or the last time I opened my

Bible. I feel miserable. To be more accurate, my spirit is miserable.

A long time ago I used to be a very strong believer and my life was full of joy. I was dependent on the Lord for almost everything. Now my life has deteriorated, spiritually and morally.

It began when I met Neil, a very attractive man. I knew that he was not for me since he was not a Christian. My stubbornness was great, however, so I started dating him and fell in love. I fooled myself by thinking that I was going to make him a Christian. The opposite has happened.

At first I refused his sexual advances, but I was weak and lonely. Instead of getting closer to God, I got closer to Neil. Little by little, he started touching me more sexually. I let him because I needed someone physically and emotionally close to me. Finally, we had sex. Now we do it often.

I am sinning. I don't know what to do. I love Neil very, very much, but I want to come back to God. I know I should break up with Neil, but I can't. It seems like I can't live without him.

I can't love people any more. I can't forgive. I can't stop lying. I can't read the Bible. I just can't be a Christian anymore.

Please help me. I am desperate. I want to come back to God, but I can't help feeling I will fail again as has happened so many times. I can't leave Neil. I love him. What if I leave Neil and

can't come back to God? I may never be able to
come back to God if you don't help me.

What a sad situation. My heart reached out to Heather
in her confusion. She can come back to God. God will forgive her, but it will mean giving up everything—including
Neil—in order that her needs might be filled by God in His
way.

I wrote Heather a long letter, encouraging her and
counseling her toward restored fellowship with God. That
information, along with the "Seven Steps to Freedom," is in
my book, *Free to Love Again.*[5]

God was thinking of our welfare when He commanded
us to "abstain from sexual immorality."[6] He loves those
who haven't abstained, and He offers a way back. Healing
can come, but avoiding the painful wounds in the first
place is much better. Saying yes and being sorry can
involve much more than we ever bargained for.

Expecting Only Time
to Heal

■ ■ ■

I remember standing in the ocean one day," a friend once told me, "calling to someone on the beach. Suddenly, an unexpected wave came crashing over me. I found myself being swept under the water and being dragged along the ocean floor with the sand biting into my hands and face."

Sometimes our past and even our present sneaks up behind us like that wave and crashes down on us; this upsets our emotional balance and may sweep us to the bottom in depression. Memories of loss, failure, and guilt bite into our emotions and inflame past wounds with as much sting as ever.

Almost all of us have emotional scars of one kind or another—painful memories of broken promises, a broken heart, or a broken love relationship. We trust someone with our heart, with the deepest secrets of our life, only to discover the person is untrustworthy. We open ourselves up only to be shut out. Sometimes we feel the shame and feelings of regret that come from the memory of using or hurting someone else. Whether the blame is primarily ours or another person's, the relationship is over and we feel empty, bitter, foolish, and alone.

To give oneself emotionally to another person and then be cut off brings deep wounds. But to give yourself completely—body, soul and spirit—and then to be abandoned can be devastating.

As I counsel with singles all over the United States, I come across thousands of wounded people, both Christians and non-Christians. I have found that a large percentage of them are experiencing an emotional earthquake within because they have loved and lost. Their lives and their dreams for the future are shattered.

As one person wrote:

> Time passes. I wait for the pain to subside. I thought time heals. When? That's the question. How long? How long till this lump dissolves from my throat? How long till I quit feeling like a hollow body walking around? Till the agony of this whole ordeal goes away? Till I forget how much I love and miss the person and yet hate, as well? I feel like I live in eternity, like this hurt will go on endlessly. Please, Time, heal me!

Time heals all wounds—or so we've heard. Yet, in reality, time by itself only dulls the pain or hides the underlying questions. Yes, healing takes time, but healing also takes more than time.

Healing Is a Process

As mentioned earlier, people today want instant gratification. This applies to our healing as well. We want our wounds healed now! We want everything to be okay now. We want quick fixes and easy answers. However, when it comes to having emotional wounds healed, the answers aren't always easy ones. The process of healing takes many steps.

Step 1: Realize That Time and Effort Are Involved

The first step toward the healing process is to resist the temptation to find a quick cure. We are foolish if we think we can rush the healing process of an emotional wound. If we do, we are likely to end up with only a superficial covering over the wound.

Although we need to allow time to work its cures, we can't passively wait for time alone to accomplish healing. We have an active part to play in the healing process ourselves. Otherwise, we will have an infected and uncared-for wound which may not heal. Taking action to help the healing is as important for an emotional wound as it is for a physical wound.

Step 2: Desire to Be Healed

Next, you need to answer the question, Do I really want to receive healing in my life? Jesus asked this same question to a man who had been an invalid for 38 years. He saw him lying down and asked him, "Do you want to get well?"[1] He tested the man's own desire for healing. Jesus put into the man's hands the power of restoration. It all depended on how much the man desired to get well.

Why wouldn't someone want to be healed? It could be because of the benefits of being afflicted. A person can become so accustomed to coping with the disadvantages of afflictions that those disadvantages eventually seem comfortable, even desirable.

For instance, Bartimaeus, the blind beggar in the Bible, was totally dependent on others. If he were healed, it would mean he would have to become responsible for his own survival. He would have to learn to work at a trade, not sit and beg all day. His reasons for not leading a more productive life would no longer be valid. People would no longer be willing to help him. Healing would mean a drastic change in his lifestyle. Yet he enthusiastically exclaimed to Jesus, "I want to regain my sight."[2]

Sometimes, clinging to emotional wounds, whether they are deserved (the consequences of past sins) or undeserved, is easier than facing the feelings that are the result of wounding experiences. Some people fear that facing their true feelings will be too much to handle. Others believe that their present misery is deserved payment for past sins instead of accepting God's forgiveness and forgiving themselves. Some withhold forgiveness by nursing a grudge in order to make the offender keep on paying for his or her offense. Sometimes we become so used to living with hurt and pain that we are afraid to live without it. If a person is healed from an emotional wound, he would no longer have excuses to keep from being more responsible and productive in life.

Therefore, before you go on to the next step in the healing process, ask yourself, *Do I truly want to be healed?* Your answer to that question will either keep you locked up in an internal prison or start the process toward freedom and wholeness.

Step 3: Allow Jesus to Help in the Healing

Realize that you need Jesus to go through the healing process with you. The prophet Isaiah describes Jesus' healing abilities in this way:

> He was despised and rejected by men, a man of sorrows, and familiar with suffering. Like one from whom men hide their faces he was despised, and we esteemed him not. Surely he took up our infirmities and carried our sorrows....But he was pierced for our transgressions, he was crushed for our iniquities; the punishment that brought us peace was upon him, and by his wounds we are healed.[3]

Here we see the Savior who not only took on the punishment for our sin but also took on a total identification with our wounds and pain. As a result, Jesus has been called the Wounded Healer.

More than anyone, Jesus sees and understands the depth of our pain and sorrow. He opens His heart and His arms to us throughout the entire process of healing. Christ is not like a friend who may listen to you pour out your confusion and pain but doesn't really understand your plight. Our Lord is not like that. He fully understands because He knows everything about you and your situation. He created you and is intimately acquainted with all your ways.[4]

Jesus understands that the way of healing is not easy. Some of the steps can be agonizing. He knows we may fail and falter along the road to our healing. Yet He is with us, coaxing us through His Holy Spirit—the great Comforter— to keep moving ahead. And Jesus is as pleased with us during the healing process, even in our failures and faltering, as a parent is with a child who is learning to walk.

We were excited when our daughter Rachel took her first steps before falling. We were just as pleased with her after she had fallen as we were while she was taking those first small steps. She, however, cried out of pain and frustration from her fall.

When I saw Rachel crying, I didn't say, "When are you ever going to learn to walk? What a failure you are! All you have to do is put one foot in front of the other! It's so easy! Now get up and do it."

Instead, when she fell, I smiled and held her because I loved her so much. I knew that walking was a learning process and falling was part of that process. "Rachel, you are doing okay. Now, honey, try again." Gradually, Rachel walked farther between falls. Paula and I picked her up each time she fell, encouraged her, and cheered her on as she tried again. I loved watching my daughter learn to walk, run, and overcome lots of other barriers.

In much the same way, God watches and understands the process of physical and emotional healing. He is pleased with us during each step of that process because He loves watching us overcome the emotional and spiritual barriers in our lives. Jesus, the Wonderful Counselor,[5] is with us and helps us as we step out and walk through the healing process.

Step 4: Face and Release Your Emotions

To move on and see true healing take place in our lives, we need to find out where we stand with our emotions. We need to identify our hidden feelings. By facing our emotions, owning up to the worst, we rob those feelings of power to keep on hurting us.

We cannot erase the past, but the pain and wreckage that is left can be healed as we face and release our emotions. When we try to keep our feelings quiet, we stop the healing process as well as our ability to give and receive forgiveness. Sometimes people think they have their negative feelings under control when actually they have only buried them alive. But these negative feelings constantly climb out of that grave.

We cannot put the past behind us as long as there are stifled tears that need to be shed and half-felt feelings that need to be experienced. We cannot fully experience God's forgiveness, forgive ourselves, or forgive others until we first face the pain.

When we are too afraid to own up to our pain—anger, hurt, shame, or guilt—and won't permit ourselves to feel it fully, we dodge the real issue of forgiveness. We need to face feelings and problems with ruthless honesty and, with God's grace, come to grips with the feelings that keep us bound and crippled. We must ask God to help us get in touch with our feelings and take responsibility for them; then we must ask God to release us from their power.

In a real sense, we need to relive the emotions from the experiences that have hurt us. Then we need to express those emotions out loud or in writing. While expressing this anger, hurt, shame, or guilt, visualize and know that the Lord's presence is with you. Keep on expressing these thoughts, feelings, and tears until you have nothing more to express. How long this will take will depend upon the depth of the wound. Remember that the Lord will not be surprised or afraid of the wording of our emotions, for He knows our deepest thoughts already. We can feel free to open up the floodgates to Him.

Sometimes this expressing of our emotions should be done with a faithful, trustworthy friend—someone to whom we can pour out our hearts, someone who will accept us in spite of our emotions and who will help us go through them. Confessing our emotions and sin with such a friend is like seeing God's love with skin on. The Lord encourages us to be open and honest with trusted Christian friends: "Therefore confess your sins to one another, and pray for one another so that you may be healed."[6]

Step 5: Receive God's Forgiveness

Before we can forgive ourselves or others fully, we must first experience God's forgiveness. His forgiveness can free us from the sin and hurt that entangle us and keep us chained in our past.

We don't need to try to pay for our own sins, nor does God want us to. By His death and sacrifice on the cross, Jesus Christ paid for our sin—not just some of our sin, but all of it. Our sin—past, present, and future—is covered under Christ's blood shed on the cross.[7]

On the day of Christ's death, He cried out from the cross, "It is finished!"[8] This statement expresses an extremely significant truth about our forgiveness. The Greek word that is used in this exclamation was primarily used in business transactions. When "it is finished" was written across a bill, it meant "paid in full." Christ was saying, by the act of dying on the cross, that our bill or debt of sin was paid in full. Therefore, we never need to pay for any of our sins. It is already finished, paid in full.

Because the price of His forgiveness has already been paid, God is ready to forgive us. We can come to Him no matter what we've done or who we are. God accepts us fully and forgives us completely. All we need to do is to accept that forgiveness freely.

To some people, God is a stern debt collector. They fail to realize what Christ accomplished on the cross. They miss the whole reason for His coming to earth. Jesus said, "It is not those who are healthy who need a physician, but those who are sick; I did not come to call the righteous, but sinners."[9] Because each of us has failed miserably to obey God, we are the reason why Jesus came. Remember, He came willingly because He loves you and me so much.

To be forgiven by God re-creates our past in the sense that His forgiveness washes us whiter than snow and lets us stand clean before Him. As we accept God's forgiveness, we can begin to experience freedom from our past. For those who have gotten involved in intimacies that should have been reserved for a spouse, God restores their emotional and spiritual virginity as they accept His forgiveness and experience His healing.

As we begin to accept and receive God's forgiveness, we begin also to take part in the next step of the healing process.

Step 6: Gain God's Perspective on Your Wounds

God has the ability to take our hurts and failures and turn them to our good and to His glory. Recognizing this is critical. Amazingly, God can work all things together for our good. Romans 8:28 says, "And we know that God causes all things to work together for good to those who love God, to those who are called according to His purpose." This *does not* mean that all things are good in themselves or that we escape the natural consequences of our actions. It *does* mean that God can somehow take all the actions and reactions of our lives, good and bad, and work them together for our ultimate good.

As you look at past relationships or whatever it is that has left emotional wounds, ask God to show you ways that He might use them in your life for good. We don't have to continue to live in despair or guilt. In Christ, we can have true hope and move forward to be used by Him to help others.

Before Simon Peter betrayed Him, Jesus said, "Simon, Simon, behold, Satan has demanded permission to sift you like wheat. But I have prayed for you, that your faith may not fail; and you, when once you have turned again, strengthen your brothers."[10] Jesus knew Peter was going to turn against Him. But Christ knew that this betrayal could be used ultimately for good in Peter's life and in the lives of others.

Our lives may look like a scrap pile, but God can build trophies from scrap piles. To gain God's perspective on your wounds, keep an eye out for how He has used or can use your pain and failures and wounds for good.

Step 7: Forgive Yourself

I found the following handwritten, unsigned note pinned to a high-school bulletin board:

To anyone,

I need help to understand what life is all about, to see the way my life should go. Does God forgive me for all my sins? I need to see that I can live the Christian life—that I can change to fit in. I want to live a whole life without always needing a man in my life.

And I have a question. Is there someone out there who will want to marry a girl who isn't a virgin? Before you answer, think about this: This girl has had intercourse before. You don't know how many guys she's had intercourse with. How do you know that after you are married, she won't go out and find someone else? Okay, maybe she said she wouldn't, but if she's had intercourse with other strange guys, why wouldn't she go out and do it again?

She is a Christian and knows what she did was wrong, but she can't block out what she did. She isn't pure anymore and never will be. That's the way it is with me. I'm not pure. I will never be pure again. Oh, why did I do what I did? Tell me, if you can. Why do people do that kind of thing?

Thank you for listening, whoever you are. Please go in peace.

As I read that girl's anguished note, my heart went out to her. Taking the step to forgive yourself can be very difficult, especially if you feel deep sorrow and guilt about your actions. Forgiving yourself, however, is essential if you are to see healing. When you forgive yourself, you become both the forgiver and the forgiven.

If we forgive ourselves for our wrong choices and actions, then we have truly accepted God's forgiveness in our hearts. And if we forgive ourselves, forgiving others will be much easier. Truly forgiving yourself because you are first forgiven by God actually gives you strength to fight Satan's attacks.

When you forgive yourself, you must be honest with yourself. It has been said that forgiving is for realists. Simply pushing failures or sin out of your mind is not forgiveness.

You can go on to one of two extremes: whipping yourself over and over or minimizing what you have done. Neither of these options helps to bring about healing.

Forgiving yourself is a process. Look at your sin honestly, accept God's forgiveness for that sin, ask Him to give you some insight on your inner makeup and needs, and then make a clear-cut decision to forgive yourself. Although forgiveness of self should be definite, you may find that you need to remind yourself of that forgiveness often until the memory of past failures no longer pulls you down. Turn negative self-talk into positive encouragement.

At the end of his life, the apostle Paul wrote to Timothy, his son in the faith. Even though he was probably over 60 years old, Paul had learned to forgive himself for his past sins because of God's grace to him.

> I thank Christ Jesus our Lord, who has given me strength, that he considered me faithful, appointing me to his service. Even though I was once a blasphemer and a persecutor and a violent man, I was shown mercy because I acted in ignorance and unbelief. The grace of our Lord was poured out on me abundantly, along with the faith and love that are in Christ Jesus. Here is a trustworthy saying that deserves full acceptance: Christ Jesus came into the world to save sinners—of whom I am the worst. But for that very reason I was shown mercy so that in me, the worst of sinners, Christ Jesus might display his unlimited patience as an example for those who would believe on him and receive eternal life.[11]

Step 8: Forgive Others

To complete the process of healing, we need to forgive the person or persons who played a part in bringing hurt and pain into our lives. Until we go through most of the other steps, however, even considering forgiving the person who wounded us may be very difficult.

Forgiving someone else does not change the other person. Forgiving others changes us. It frees us from the past and from our need to try to seek revenge, either physically or mentally. If we don't forgive that other person, we will be stuck on "getting even."

Our minds will continue to replay the painful incident, not with what actually happened but with what we would have liked to have said or done differently. This keeps us hooked into the hate and the pain. Forgiveness turns off this mental replay and releases us from painful memories that keep our wounds open and festering.

Hidden hate and anger affect not only us, but sooner or later, they also affect our other relationships. An unforgiving spirit eventually produces bitterness toward anything that vaguely reminds us of the painful experience. This spills over, sometimes subtly and sometimes obviously, into our relationships—even with those we love. In the end, bitterness, not the pain and hurt, will destroy us.

How then do we forgive another person? See your own forgiveness before God. Through Christ's forgiveness we have had a tremendous debt to God erased. God has released us from having to pay that debt of sin against us. But often we are like the unmerciful servant Jesus talked about in Matthew 18:23-35.

In this parable, Jesus tells about a servant of the king who owed the king ten thousand talents—worth several million dollars today. To settle the account, the king was going to sell the man and his whole family into slavery and sell all his possessions. When the man fell on his knees and begged for more time to repay the debt, the king responded with compassion and cancelled out his debt entirely. This part of the story can be likened to the debt of sin that we owed God.

But what did the former debtor do then?

> But that slave went out and found one of his fellow slaves who owed him a hundred denarii [about a few dollars]; and he seized him and began to choke him, saying, "Pay back what you owe." So his fellow slave fell to the ground and began to entreat him, saying, "Have patience with me and I will repay you."[12]

The man refused his own debtor's plea. Instead, he ended up having him thrown in jail.

When the king heard about this, he was furious. "I had mercy on you to cancel the huge debt you owed to me! But you did not show any mercy for a tiny debt another man owed you" (paraphrased). The king severely punished the wicked servant.

Then Christ makes this statement: "This is how my heavenly Father will treat each of you unless you forgive your brother from your heart."[13]

What a perfect illustration of what we do when we refuse to forgive others after God has completely cancelled out our debt. Any refusal within our hearts to forgive others puts us in the same category as this unmerciful servant.

No matter how much someone has hurt us, their wrong cannot compare with the debt we owed God for our sin. The other person's offense toward us is very small in comparison. God has shown us complete forgiveness and mercy. In light of this, how can we have an unforgiving, unmerciful heart toward those who have sinned against us?

Forgiveness of others is not easy, especially if the wound is deep. To forgive completely takes time. But when we get this comparison in perspective, the way of forgiveness is easier. While focusing on the pain that someone else has caused us, we need to ask the question, What did I do to hurt the other person? Many times we are not totally blameless in a situation. We need to look honestly not only at what the other person has done to us but also at what we may have done to that person.

Forgiving another person is easier if we have some understanding of the person and what his or her needs are. If we look beyond the behavior that hurt us and see that person's inner needs, we can begin to see the situation more objectively. This enables us to see the person apart from the wrong he or she has done to us and makes forgiving him or her much easier.

You will know you are beginning to forgive someone when you begin to wish him or her well and truly want the best for his or her life. This is very difficult to do when we are still bitter.

Through forgiving others we can let go of the bitterness and anger that keep us knotted up inside. Only in forgiveness can we find freedom from the pain, the hurt, and the misery that can come our way in life.

As we go through the healing process, we can begin to experience restoration and freedom from the pain of the past. God will take our broken hearts, broken lives, and broken promises and restore us to being whole persons again. Then He enables us to bring healing to other people's lives. The God of hope and mercy is in the business of taking broken people and putting them together again.

Gary Rosberg sums it up nicely: "As forgiveness is given, both the giver and the receiver experience emotional relief. The pressure is off, the pain begins to subside and healing starts."[14]

Part Three

Becoming the Right Person

13

Build Qualities
That Attract

■ ■ ■

After dating many women, I came up with the general character traits of the woman I wanted to become my wife. I called her my GOIA woman. Through experience, I had learned what I liked best. I was not looking for items to check off a list, but for general character qualities. I began to pray for this woman even before I met her. I prayed that she would be described by these words:

G—Godly. She didn't have to be a super-spiritual giant, but I desired a woman who would have a loving, personal relationship with God. I knew that she would probably relate to God in different ways than I did, but I just wanted a woman who had a strong, growing faith in Christ.

O—Outgoing. I tend to be on the quiet side, although some people find that hard to believe. On dates I enjoyed listening. When I dated a woman who was also a quiet listener, we had a quiet date. Silence reigned. I needed a woman who was more outgoing than myself, one who would make the conversation lively and draw me out.

I—Intelligent. I hoped that the woman for me would enjoy conversing on a variety of topics. She didn't have to have a Ph.D., but I hoped that she would want to continually expand her mind and motivate me to keep growing intellectually.

231

A—Attractive. I wasn't looking for a cover-girl knockout. But I was interested in finding someone I enjoyed looking at. I didn't care what anyone else thought of her as long as I thought she was attractive.

Through the many years of being single, I realized that having general ideas of what you want in a spouse is okay. But don't keep a long list of specifics. Many married people have told me, "The person God finally gave me is so different from what I anticipated." Don't get locked into a set of picky characteristics that drastically limit your choices. Ask God for general qualities you want in a spouse and let Him fill in the details.

Our Own Character

As I looked for my GOIA woman, I was very aware that I needed to develop characteristics that would make me attractive and personally fulfilling to her. Here are two questions to ask yourself:

- When I meet the person who has all the characteristics I want in a spouse, will he or she want me?

- Do I have the characteristics they are looking for?

A woman I once dated gave me an interesting thought. "When you get right down to it," she said, "it's not the outside that ultimately is important. It's the heart, personality, and character." How wise she was. As Christian men and women, we need to build inner characteristics that are magnetic, that appeal not just to the opposite sex but to people in general.

God's Character

Attractive qualities originate in God. He is the most attractive of all. His character is filled with all that is perfect and beautiful. Because Christ is God, the qualities He displays show what the divine nature of God is like. One of the benefits of following Christ is that God is making us and molding us to become like Him.

> And we know that God causes all things to work together for good to those who love God, to those who are called according to His purpose. For those whom He foreknew, He also predestined to become conformed to the image of His Son, so that He would be the firstborn among many brethren.[1]

The potential for Christlikeness is unlimited. Due to the indwelling of the Holy Spirit, we can trust God, by faith, to produce in us all the beautiful characteristics of the Lord Jesus. Our motivation is to reflect His character to the world.

> Walk in a manner worthy of the Lord, to please Him in all respects, bearing fruit in every good work and increasing in the knowledge of God; strengthened with all power, according to His glorious might, for the attaining of all steadfastness and patience.[2]

As a result of pleasing God, we will become attractive to others, especially to those who want to honor the Lord in their lives. We can study God's Word diligently and apply it in such a way as to develop the characteristics and behavior God wants for us. The amazing thing is that the Lord has not left us on our own to do the impossible. Rather, as we believe in Him, He will give us the desire and the power to do His will. The apostle Paul acknowledged this when he wrote, "For it is God who is at work in you, both to will and to work for His good pleasure."[3]

The Fruit of the Spirit

The Holy Spirit is the means by which God produces godly character in us. As a tree produces fruit after its kind, so God is producing His fruit in us so that we will become like Him in our character, attitudes, and behavior.

"But the fruit of the Spirit is love, joy, peace, patience, kindness, goodness, faithfulness, gentleness, self-control."[4] These are the nine characteristics the Spirit wants to produce in us. Therefore, if we pray that the Lord will develop these traits in us, and actively endeavor to mature in these areas, God will cause us to become the attractive persons He wants us to be.

As we focus attention on each fruit, remember that God's will and purpose for us is to possess all of them. Don't be like Benjamin Franklin. He chose 13 admirable traits that he desired for his life. He worked on producing one each week. He was somewhat successful the first week on developing trait number one. As he was concentrating on the second trait the next week, however, his efforts to maintain the first trait failed. He couldn't succeed in more than one trait at a time. Frustrated and defeated, he finally gave up.

Don't give up. We have the Holy Spirit to produce and develop these attractive qualities in us. We are not left alone to depend upon ourselves. Actively trust Him to provide power in your life each day to develop these qualities.

Love

Much has been written on this subject, and I have already discussed many aspects of love. But one area needs reemphasizing: Learn to love yourself.

We are made in the image of God with unique strengths and weaknesses. Although the greatest commandment, Jesus said, was to love God with your whole being, the second one was to "love your neighbor as yourself."[5] Love what God has made you.

A healthy self-esteem is a great gift to give someone in dating and marriage. If you enjoy who you are, you will be willing to accept your neighbor, your friends, and the person you are dating. Base your self-esteem neither on circumstances nor on fleeting feelings but on God's great love for you. He is the greatest example of genuine sacrificial love.

As He has done for you, take every opportunity to do loving things for other people. Go out of your way to help meet people's needs even if they don't appreciate your efforts. Christ went to the cross to demonstrate His love for us. To what lengths will you go to express your love for others?

If you would like to read more about a Bible-based, healthy self-image, you can do so in my book *Building a Biblical Self-Image*.[6] It will help you take your eyes off of your inadequacies and focus on what God created you to be.

Joy

To delight in the Lord is to be filled with appreciation for all that He is: His power, holiness, justice, mercy, greatness, and love. He is the object of joy, and the more you learn about His attributes, the more your heart will be filled with gladness. The prophet Jeremiah exclaimed, "When your words came, I ate them; they were my joy and my heart's delight, for I bear your name, O LORD God Almighty."[7] So daily feast upon the Scriptures and allow your heart to be flooded with gladness.

Look at the positive side. Nothing is so dull and boring as listening to someone complain all the time. The apostle Paul could have had a defeated attitude about being in prison for four years. On the contrary, while in prison, he told the Philippian church, "Rejoice in the Lord always; again I will say, rejoice!"[8]

How do you react when the pressures of life appear to be crushing you? What reaction do you have in the midst of great disappointments or emotional pain? On the way to the cross, Christ had in His mind the "joy set before Him."[9]

Our salvation was in His heart as He faced an agonizing and painful death. He had joy in the midst of pain. We can also. Be encouraged. Praise the Lord always. People want to be around a joyful person.

Peace

We need a calm mind and stomach in this fast-paced world. Whenever people were fretful in the Scriptures, God would say, "Be strong and courageous. Do not be terrified; do not be discouraged, for the LORD your God will be with you wherever you go."[10] Acknowledging the presence of God is the best antidote for anxious thoughts and feelings.

When we feel lonely or hurt, we usually withdraw into our little shell. We feel safe there, but the loneliness increases because we are alone. Be willing to take risks in relationships, in developing the Relationship Star, and in meeting new people. Be bold in reaching out to others. Let Christ's peace fill your mind.[11]

Make prayer your constant attitude. Rest in the power of the Lord to work out all things according to His will. Become a peacemaker in relationships and endeavor to bring harmony between people. Others are attracted to someone who is calm in the midst of stormy circumstances. "Let the peace of Christ rule in your hearts."[12]

Patience

I saw a cartoon in a magazine that pictured a little girl kneeling beside her bed and praying. "Dear Lord, I ask for patience, and I want it right now!"

Isn't that like us? We find it difficult to wait for anything. But God is not unnerved. He is totally in control.
Nothing takes Him by surprise. He is always on time, never
too late and never too early.

Be patient with your singleness. He knows the biolog-
ical clock is ticking. He understands your deepest desires
for a spouse. Ask God to give you His perspective on time.
You need to develop the kind of endurance that marathon
runners have. Mile after mile they plod along, focusing
their minds on the unseen finish line. Allow the Holy Spirit
to strengthen your endurance. Hope in God will carry you
through the long nights and the frustrating days.

If there are problems that have not been resolved, even
after months or years, keep trusting God's power to work
things out. If your singleness continually disturbs you, per-
severe under the pressure. If your job is boring or tedious,
make the best of that day for God's glory and leave the
future up to Him. "Those who wait for the LORD will gain
new strength; they will mount up with wings like eagles,
they will run and not get tired, they will walk and not
become weary." [13]

Kindness

Have you noticed that God gives us commands that are
difficult, if not impossible, for us to obey? When Christ
talked about our attitudes and actions toward people who
are antagonistic or apathetic toward us, He told us to be
gracious toward them.

> But love your enemies, do good to them, and
> lend to them without expecting to get anything
> back. Then your reward will be great, and you
> will be sons of the Most High, because he is kind
> to the ungrateful and wicked. Be merciful, just as
> your Father is merciful. [14]

Don't let your tongue tear people apart or cut people down. Be gracious in your speech and actions.

Cultivate hospitality. Invite people for dinner and try your skills at cooking. Be openhearted to new people who attend your single-adult meetings. Make someone else's day by being loving and pleasant, even if he or she has been obnoxious or withdrawn.

Goodness

Pick up any newspaper or news magazine and you will read about how wickedly and selfishly people treat one another. Our world is full of wars, hatred, strife, and destruction. In a similar situation, the psalmist said, "I would have despaired unless I had believed that I would see the goodness of the LORD in the land of the living."[15] In a darkened world of sin, God's goodness shines like a thousand suns. The word "good" refers to moral integrity and righteous character. Let God's character shine through you. When the person you are dating wants to step across God's moral boundary, take a stand on the side of purity. Be ethical and above reproach in all your dealings with people. God is a just God and wants us to be honorable in everything.

Paul admonishes us, "Instruct them to do good, to be rich in good works, to be generous and ready to share, storing up for themselves the treasure of a good foundation for the future, so that they may take hold of that which is life indeed."[16]

Faithfulness

Trustworthiness is a lost value in our society. Many people are out to get ahead no matter what it takes. People who will keep their word and do what they say they will do are hard to find. Rare is the individual who sticks with a friend through all contrary circumstances, especially the ones that call for personal sacrifice.

But God is faithful. He is unwavering in His commitment to us, even when we fail Him. "If we are faithless, He remains faithful, for He cannot deny Himself."[17] His trustworthiness is always certain in uncertain times.

Through the power of the Holy Spirit, become a person of your word. If you commit yourself to something, carry through your promise without excuses or negligence or quitting. Show people that you can be counted on by doing quality work. Don't cut corners or slack off. If you do prove undependable, humble yourself and admit your mistakes. Don't rationalize your sins. People will see right through dishonesty. If you are a fake, others will never trust you. Be genuine and earn their confidence in you.

Gentleness

In a world where "power" means to crush the competition, gentleness and sensitivity are considered weaknesses—characteristics of losers. But look at the way Christ treated people. Rome was in power at that time and ruled the world with an iron fist. Romans valued military strength above everything else. But Rome was destroyed long ago—its mighty power was decimated. Today Christ's gentle love still draws people to the Cross. Which value do you want to characterize your life—power or gentleness?

Read Christ's convictions about this issue in Matthew 20:20-28.

Have you ever watched parents hold a newborn baby? They are gentle, considerate, helpful, loving, and tender. The apostle Paul said that this was the way he treated people: "But we proved to be gentle among you, as a nursing mother tenderly cares for her own children. Having so fond an affection for you, we were well-pleased to impart to you not only the gospel of God but also our own lives, because you had become very dear to us."[18] He went on to say, "For you know that we dealt with each of you as a father deals with his own children, encouraging, comforting and urging you to live lives worthy of God, who calls you into his kingdom and glory."[19] Gentleness is not only being tender but being strong for what is right. In a dating relationship, express your convictions in a gentle manner, not harshly or with a sarcastic attitude.

Take the initiative to forgive and seek reconciliation when you feel you have been wronged or misunderstood. Let the Lord cleanse your mind of any bitterness you may harbor. Learn to comfort with the same comfort you have received from the Lord.

Self-Control

Our imaginations love to run wild. We play with the temptations to cross moral boundaries. Our appetite craves all kinds of food that are not good for us. We enjoy being lazy and spreading rumors about people. Jealousy can grab us in an instant and a sharp tongue can easily get us into trouble. In countless ways we see attitudes in ourselves that are not pleasing to God. Temptations constantly hit us in our weak spots.

How can we handle all these powerful attitudes and emotions? Without God we are uncontrollable. But that is just the point, for self-control is really Spirit-control. Only He can channel our energies and tame our wildness. He doesn't stifle us or put us in a straitjacket. Ironically, when He controls us, we are set free.

To become disciples of the Lord is to place ourselves under His authority and to be closely yoked to Him.[20] His power is available to set us free from anything that binds or enslaves us. He can break the chains of bad habits or addictions to ungodly practices.

"Discipline" is not a popular word in our society today, but it is the key word for being a disciple. Obedience to Christ shows our deep love for Him, and self-control shows our loyalty to His will. As we consistently come to Him for direction and strength, we learn to deal with the emotions and habits that pull us down. To increase your self-control, establish a daily devotional time of Bible study and prayer. Develop the art of stopping and thinking before reacting negatively to circumstances. You can control your temper with the power Christ gives to those who trust Him.[21] Paul understood all this:

> Do you not know that those who run in a race all run, but only one receives the prize? Run in such a way that you may win....Therefore I run in such a way, as not without aim; I box in such a way, as not beating the air; but I discipline my body and make it my slave, so that after I have preached to others, I myself will not be disqualified.[22]

All these qualities are produced by abiding in the vine of Christ.[23] Fruit grows when it is intimately connected with the source of life. If we receive our spiritual life from the Holy Spirit, we will develop all these traits.

One caution. Don't expect overnight results. Some areas may be easy for you to change; others may be difficult. But none is impossible. Producing fruit is a process that takes time. You may take three steps forward and two backward. Don't get discouraged with temporary setbacks. Keep moving ahead with faith and confidence.

The Attractiveness of Praise

My favorite passage throughout my single years was Psalm 34. It begins, "I will extol the LORD at all times (except when I'm single)." Wrong. That's not the way it goes.

> I will extol the LORD at all times;
> His praise will always be on my lips.
> My soul will boast in the LORD;
> Let the afflicted hear and rejoice.
> Glorify the LORD with me;
> Let us exalt His name together.[24]

The solution to living through the ups and downs of our lives is to praise the Lord. Why? Because we can praise God all the time. "I will extol the LORD at *all times*." The verse does not say, "except in certain disappointing situations."

When David wrote this psalm, he was in a tight situation where he could have been killed.[25] He faked insanity so that everyone would leave him alone. He was left in the wilderness to wander as a crazed man. In the midst of this ordeal, he said, "His praise will always be on my lips." Why? Because God Almighty was still on His throne. He always knows how to work things out. Nothing takes God by surprise or defeats Him.

We know that God loves us and knows what is best for us at all times. Even when we are in the pit of despondency, God knows how to transform our lives. He knows how to raise us up and to put a new smile on our faces.

David said that we should praise the Lord on our own. "My soul will boast in the LORD." The word "boasting" in this verse conveys the attitude, *I'm proud of my God and I'll show it*. This is good boasting because the focus is on God and not on prideful self. Jesus Christ said the "mouth speaks from that which fills [the] heart."[26] Joyful praise comes from the overflow of a life filled with the goodness of the Lord.

David also exhorted us to praise Him not only on our own but also with other people. "Let the afflicted hear and rejoice. Glorify the LORD with me; let us exalt his name together."[27]

The closer you walk with God, the more refreshing, exhilarating, and exciting life becomes. You won't be alone. Other people will join you and get in on the action of trusting God and exalting Him. As He overflows your heart, others will want to enjoy the Lord with you. Glorifying God is contagious. Maybe that is why Psalm 34 was my favorite when I was single.

Wrong Goals

Many singles focus on the wrong goals. One of these is pursuing marriage. They push the Panic Button and go on the hunt for someone to marry.

When Emery was a university student, he said that he witnessed both men and women pursuing the wrong goals in dating. The men were often annoyed and intimidated by women who took dating "too seriously." They wanted "to figure out if the two of us could get married after only a few dates." However, Emery says "it goes both ways," and he knew men who would become possessive over the women they dated early on in the relationship. Both men and women adopted the attitude that if they didn't find someone while they were a university student, then they "might never find someone."

Often many singles form unrealistic expectations early in the relationship. Perhaps you have done it as well, thinking, *Okay, I just met so-and-so at a party last night. Maybe that person will become interested in me and we'll eventually get together.* Or you remember someone you once dated, perhaps your first love, and you dream of getting back together.

The problem with living in such a fantasy world is that when you come back to reality, you are frustrated. The more unrealistic expectations you form, the more frustrated you become. You think you have to get married in order to be completely happy.

Another wrong goal is trying to find the perfect match to your ideal. Whenever you meet someone, you immediately ask yourself, *Is this the right one? Let's see, I have my list of requirements for a potential spouse right here. This person checks out on qualifications numbers one, two, and five. But three, four, six, seven, and eight...no. This person doesn't measure up to enough of the qualifications. Sorry.*

The frustration is that no one will ever measure up to your list completely. The list adds tremendous pressure to finding the right one. It's hard to relax when meeting someone if the list is there in the forefront of your mind.

Right Goals

What does the Lord think about this? Instead of pursuing marriage, pursue the Lord. "I sought the LORD, and he answered me; he delivered me from all my fears."[28] Pursuing the Lord is exciting. When you seek Him, the pain of not having someone that you pursued for marriage begins to dissipate. He delivers you from the fear of never getting married as well as from other fears.

God's viewpoint is to pursue love, not marriage. He has given you your single years to learn how to love faithfully, to learn how to give yourself to someone else in friendship, to learn how to become the right person, to learn how to walk with the Lord, to learn how to be sensitive to another person's needs, to learn how the opposite sex thinks and feels, and to learn how to communicate your heart to others.

Singles tell me that they are looking for a spouse who can really help them walk with God. But if you are dependent upon someone else to help you know God intimately, you have a problem. Your walk with God is supposed to be an independent, personal relationship with Him. It is not to be a vicarious, second-hand relationship through a spouse or friend. Someone of the opposite sex who meets your specifications for godliness is not going to want to be married to a spiritual clinging vine or to a flat tire that needs to be pumped up all the time. Each of us is responsible for our own walk with the Lord. So get to know Christ now.

The right goal for singles is to become the right person. If you seek to be the right person, God will take care of finding the right spouse for you according to His purpose for your life.

The Single Adventure

Life is a daily adventure with the Lord, married or single. Each day, a step at a time, we need to walk with Him in faithfulness, trust, and surrender. When we commit our way to Him, He guides our steps. We have a great God. He is infinitely creative and will meet you in your deepest needs and give you a quality of life that is superior to anything you could design on your own.

The single life can be an exciting one that attracts other people to you but only when you entrust yourself to the Lord each day. Christ and you are an unbeatable combination!

Keep on the Right Path to the Right One

■ ■ ■

It had been a long five-month trip to 22 countries throughout Africa, Asia, and the Middle East, assisting the international staff of Campus Crusade for Christ in their ministries. Finally, I arrived in Manila, in the Philippines, my final stop before heading across the Atlantic toward home. I was 28 years old, tired, lonely, and hadn't had a date in over five months.

Around dusk, I was walking through the art district of Manila toward my hotel. Suddenly, before I realized what was happening, a gorgeous woman stepped out from between two buildings and walked toward me. She grabbed my arm and said, "Hi, how are you tonight?"

I was taken completely off guard. "I'd like to give you a good time," she said. "Why don't we go to my apartment and have some fun?"

I had always assumed that prostitutes who walked the streets would be ugly, but this one was attractive. She probably seemed especially so because I had not experienced a woman's touch for many months.

A battle raged within me. I would have loved just to be cared for and to feel a woman's warmth, yet the thought also hammered in my mind, *This is dangerous. Don't play with fire!*

She saw my hesitation and said, "Come on. My husband is on a long trip. He won't be back for weeks."

"No, I can't," were the only words that I could weakly get out of my mouth. I was still struggling with my thoughts and emotions.

"Let's go," she said. "I know how to give you a really good time."

"No, I can't," I replied again. But in my heart I knew I was wavering. I knew that the desire for a woman was very strong. Yet, I wanted to obey God's Word. What a dilemma!

Standing on the sidewalk, as I still struggled in my mind, the woman said, "Here's a taxi. Let's go. It will be a good time."

Weakly, I replied again, "No, I can't."

Finally, she stopped pulling on my arm and said, "Why?" That little hesitation on her part gave me greater courage to say what was really on my mind. Even though I wanted that warmth and wanted a woman to hold, I knew it was wrong. Even though no one in the whole world would know that I had been with a prostitute, I would know—and my God would know. The memory would burn like acid in my soul.

"Because I know Jesus Christ," I blurted out.

She let go of my arm, backed away a couple of steps, and looked at me with horror in her eyes. "Are you a priest?" she asked.

"No, I am not!" Then with all the courage that I could muster, I said boldly, "I know Jesus Christ!"

Then I shouted, "I know Jesus Christ!"

Then I screamed, "I know Jesus Christ!"

She became so frightened that she turned and ran away. I quickly went back to my hotel room, shaken to the core of my being. I had come so close. I dropped to my knees beside the bed and wept uncontrollably before God. The temptation had been so strong to go along with that woman. To think I had played around with fire and had almost been burned. Over and over again I cried, "Thank You, God, for Your strength! Thank You for the power of just saying the name of Jesus Christ! Thank You, Lord, that You gave me the courage to resist. You protected me! I had no one else to depend upon but You, and You did not fail me."

Lonely Places

For the next 14 years I continued to be single. Everyone has struggles in life. As a single man, I had my own particular set. I felt the pain of loneliness often. Oh, yes, I had roommates and lots of friends, but I struggled with not having a woman to share my life. These feelings cropped up in a number of different situations.

One was in airports. It happened the same way many times. Whenever I came back from speaking at meetings and got off the plane, a crowd of people would be waiting outside the security area to greet the arriving passengers. There would be lots of hugging and kissing. Little children would run up to people near me and yell, "Mommy, Daddy." But no one was there to greet me and hug me. I had to walk through the middle of that crowd of happy people. I felt the pain of being alone.

Another place where I had a hard time was in motel rooms. I was constantly traveling. Besides taking overseas trips in my 20s, I began speaking and teaching on university campuses throughout America in my 30s and 40s. The hardest thing for me was to address hundreds of people at one of my lectures and then afterward go back to my motel room by myself. The deafening silence of those four walls would close in on me. It was painful to be the only occupant of that room.

The other place that I struggled emotionally was when I was an assistant pastor of a church for four years in my mid-30s. Each week I worked hard preparing my sermon. I loved the challenge. On Sunday the whole church seemed to be filled with happy, smiling families. Parents would drop their kids off for Sunday school and then attend church. After the church service ended, they would all get together with their families and go home together. Once again, it would hit me, *No one is going home with me. I don't have a family.*

Traveling itself produced a fight within me. Often on my speaking trips, I would see marvelous scenery or witness the amazing power of God in people's lives as they responded to the presentations I gave. I wanted to share those beautiful events and the feelings they produced in the depths of my soul, but there was no one to share them with. I could always talk with the people I visited, but at each place the people were different. With no woman to share my deep thoughts and the beauty of life, I felt robbed of companionship.

Jokes and Formulas

Loneliness wasn't my only struggle. People and their comments were, too. Some would joke about my single state, but their words were like daggers in my heart.

- "Why isn't a nice guy like you married?"
- "Are you afraid to take responsibility?"
- "Maybe you're just too picky. Maybe you should stop looking for just the perfect one."
- "Aren't you interested in women? Are you gay?"
- "What are you waiting for?"

Other people, newly married, would enthusiastically give me their advice for getting married. But one person's formula may be another person's frustration. Comments such as these were common:

- "When I finally gave up everything to God, then, very quickly afterward, God brought the right one along."

- "Right after I learned a big lesson God wanted to teach me, He brought me my spouse."

- "When I stopped looking, then the Lord brought the person to me."

- "When I finally came to grips with my singleness and said, 'Yes, I am willing to be single for the rest of my life,' then God brought the right one along."

These formulas may work for some people, but they didn't work for me. I had sincerely given my life to God when I was in college. I had served Him on the staff of Campus Crusade for Christ for more than 16 years. I had been an assistant pastor for four years. What did these people who married in their 20s know about life that I didn't know? Why were they married, and I was single? In reality, I had not found any woman with whom I wanted to live the rest of my life. I dated lots of women, but none of them interested me. Those formulas were not the answer.

The Right Path

I had my ups and downs as a single person. But I discovered that certain things kept me on the right path.

The first was *the Bible*. It gave me a strong foundation for my life. I learned to stand on the eternal truth of God's Word, no matter what my feelings were or what circumstances confronted me. The Lord Jesus had called me to obey. "If anyone loves Me, he will keep My word..." (John 14:23). I couldn't go wrong trying to follow God's command to live a righteous life. The Scriptures became my guidebook for living.

The second was *God Himself*. Relating to the Lord was a source of joy and comfort. Prayer became for me a conversation with the God I loved. The rest of John 14:23 says, "...and My Father will love him, and We will come to him, and make Our abode with him." Openly and honestly, I learned to tell Him all my thoughts and feelings. He was the only lover I had, and I poured out my soul to Him. I developed a committed spirit toward the Lord to follow Him no matter what it cost me. I made a lot of mistakes, but through the struggles I found a certain sense of confidence in Him; I knew He would never leave me or forsake me.[1]

The third was *a group of friends*. Friendship gave me caring companions. They became my family. Wherever I traveled, I made friends and spent my spare time with them. When I came home, my roommates and the nine men in my CELL group that I wrote about earlier encouraged me greatly.

The fourth was *a ministry*. Nothing is more fulfilling than meeting the needs of other people. The goal of my life was not to get married or to establish a home. It was to glorify God with my life and talents. My overriding desire was to give my energy to help people to commit themselves to Christ and live dynamic, godly lives. Getting involved in helping others shifted my focus off myself. When I was concerned about their problems, I was less concerned about my problems. I was a lot happier that way.

The last was an assortment of *interesting activities*. These expand a person's mind and make life fun. Being single provided me with the time to become involved in a variety of hobbies and sports. I had the time and resources to do lots of things my married friends could not do. To name two, I traveled around the world twice and learned to fly single-engine airplanes.

Why?

With all of these, of course, there were still the "why" questions that I couldn't answer. Why did my older brother Herb get married at 23 and my younger brother Bob at 22? How about me, Lord?

When I turned 40, I still did not have a wife or even a viable prospect. Some wonderful female friends of mine were in their 30s and unmarried. They were wonderful (Godly, Outgoing, Intelligent, Attractive) women who loved Christ. Why weren't they married? Other friends got married in their early to mid-20s. Why do some get married and others not? I did not have answers for these burning questions. But I turned to God's Word for His direction again and again.

I clung to a promise in Psalm 37: "Trust in the LORD, and do good; dwell in the land and cultivate faithfulness. Delight yourself in the LORD; and He will give you the desires of your heart. Commit your way to the LORD, trust also in Him, and He will do it."[2]

This promise of God kept me strong in Him. I did not know when or how He would answer. It was His choice. My responsibility was to do good, to trust Him, and to be faithful. I knew that He always wanted the best for me.

Finally, in the forty-first autumn of my life, I felt I was finally building a relationship with a wonderful woman who might possibly be the one. Paula invited me to her parents' house for Thanksgiving. However, after two days of being there, I felt discouraged. Our relationship seemed as if it were on rocky ground.

The following morning, I was sitting by a window in my motel room reading the Scriptures and asking God why things were falling apart just when I thought I had at last found my GOIA woman that I could really love. As I pored over the Scriptures in my anxiety, I came across the book of the prophet Habakkuk. Everything had gone wrong during his time, and it looked as if his whole nation would be utterly destroyed by an invading army. But he turned in faith to God and said:

> Though the fig tree does not bud,
> and there are no grapes on the vines,
> though the olive crop fails
> and the fields produce no food,
> though there are not sheep in the pen
> and no cattle in the stalls,
> yet I will rejoice in the LORD,
> I will be joyful in God my savior.
> The Sovereign LORD is my strength;
> he makes my feet like the feet of a deer,
> he enables me to go on the heights.[3]

In my tears and confusion I cried out to God, "Oh Lord, even if Paula would never love me, and I would remain single all the rest of my life, I submit my heart to You. Christ, You are my God, and You are in control."

Later that day, as Paula and I talked about our relationship, I realized that I had been mistaken about her actions and intentions. Even though it all had been a misunderstanding, God had used this situation to clarify my motives. Whether He ever gave me a wife, I had reaffirmed my total commitment to Him.

Two months later I asked Paula to marry me. I was delighted and ecstatic when she answered, "Yes!" During the next four months leading up to our wedding, I pondered the question, Why did God wait so long to give me a wife? I didn't have an answer. I was still confused.

On our honeymoon, while relaxing on the beach one day, I looked off across the ocean contemplating this question. Paula interrupted my thoughts and asked, "What are you thinking about?"

"Oh, nothing," I replied.

"Now, come on, really, what are you thinking about?" she asked.

"Paula," I said, "for months I have struggled with the question, Why has God waited 42 years to finally give me a wife?"

Without a moment's hesitation, she replied, "I know!"

Startled, I exclaimed, "You know?"

"Sure," she said, "if God had brought you someone sooner, it wouldn't have been me! I wasn't ready."

That was a simple yet profound answer. God knows the whys for each of us, and He is sovereign. For me, He had been preparing the right woman and the right time all along.

Relax! Enjoy life God's way—He is in control.

Notes

Chapter 1—The Search for a Love Worthy of Your Life
1. C. S. Lewis, *The Four Loves* (New York: Harcourt Brace Jovanovich, Inc., 1960), 11-12.

Chapter 2—The Foundation for a Lasting Love
1. Proverbs 17:17
2. Matthew 7:3,5
3. Proverbs 27:9

Chapter 3—Components of Oneness
1. Philippians 2:1-2
2. 2 Corinthians 6:14-15
3. Mark 6:34
4. Matthew 14:14
5. Romans 15:5-6
6. Philippians 2:3-4
7. Philippians 2:5-7 (NIV)

Chapter 4—Your Social Life: Having Real Fun
1. Ephesians 5:25
2. Ephesians 5:33
3. Romans 12:9
4. Romans 12:9
5. Romans 12:10-11
6. Romans 12:12-13
7. Colossians 4:6

Chapter 5—Your Mental Life: Discovering How You Think
1. 1 Peter 3:8-9
2. Psalm 103:12
3. Micah 7:19 (NIV)

4. Matthew 6:12 (NIV)
5. Ephesians 2:8-9

Chapter 6—Your Emotional Life: Understanding Your Feelings

1. Matthew 1:18-25
2. Galatians 6:2
3. Ecclesiastes 4:9-10

Chapter 7—Your Physical Life: Expressing Love Creatively

1. 1 Corinthians 6:9-10
2. 1 Corinthians 6:11
3. 1 Thessalonians 2:8
4. 1 Corinthians 6:12
5. 1 Corinthians 6:13-15
6. 1 Corinthians 6:16-18
7. 1 Corinthians 6:19-20
8. 1 Thessalonians 4:3-5
9. 1 Thessalonians 4:6-8
10. 2 Timothy 2:22
11. Matthew 22:37,39
12. 1 Timothy 4:7-8
13. Philippians 4:8 (NIV)

Chapter 8—Your Spiritual Life: Exploring Your Souls

1. Genesis 2:18
2. Genesis 2:24
3. Matthew 19:6
4. Ephesians 5:18-21
5. Ephesians 5:28-32
6. Ephesians 5:21
7. Ephesians 5:22
8. Galatians 3:28
9. Psalms 62:5
10. Proverbs 21:1
11. Dick Purnell, *A Personal Experiment in Faith-Building* (Cary, NC: Dick Purnell Communications, 2001).
12. 2 Corinthians 6:14-15 (NIV)
13. Dick Purnell, *Growing Closer to God* (Cary, NC: Dick Purnell Communications, 2002).

Chapter 9—Shutting Off Transparency

1. John 17:23,26 (NIV)
2. Acts 20:35

Chapter 10—Pressing for Instant Intimacy

1. 1 John 4:10-12 (NIV)

2. Jeremiah 31:3
3. Romans 5:6-10
4. 2 Thessalonians 1:8-9
5. 1 John 1:9
6. John 3:16
7. Romans 6:23; Ephesians 2:8-9; 1 John 5:10-13
8. Hebrews 12:6-11

Chapter 11—Saying Yes and Being Sorry

1. "Sexually Transmitted Diseases Treatment Guidelines 2002," *Morbidity and Mortality Weekly Report*, May (2002), 3.
2. STD Treatment Guidelines, 3.
3. *The Medical Institute for Sexual Health Advisory*, June (2002), 1.
4. STD Treatment Guidelines, 2.
5. Dick Purnell, *Free to Love Again* (Nashville: Thomas Nelson, 1995).
6. 1 Thessalonians 4:3

Chapter 12—Expecting Only Time to Heal

1. John 5:6 (NIV)
2. Mark 10:51
3. Isaiah 53:3-5 (NIV)
4. Psalm 139
5. Isaiah 9:6
6. James 5:16
7. Hebrews 10:10-18
8. John 19:30
9. Mark 2:17
10. Luke 22:31-32
11. 1 Timothy 1:12-16 (NIV)
12. Matthew 18:28-29
13. Matthew 18:35 (NIV)
14. Gary Rosberg, *Dr. Rosberg's Do-It-Yourself Relationship Mender* (Wheaton, IL: Tyndale House Publishers, 1995), 239.

Chapter 13—Build Qualities That Attract

1. Romans 8:28-29
2. Colossians 1:10-11
3. Philippians 2:13
4. Galatians 5:22-23
5. Matthew 22:39
6. Dick Purnell, *Building a Biblical Self-Image* (Cary, NC: Dick Purnell Communications, 2003).
7. Jeremiah 15:16 (NIV)
8. Philippians 4:4
9. Hebrews 12:2
10. Joshua 1:9 (NIV)

11. John 14:27
12. Colossians 3:15
13. Isaiah 40:31
14. Luke 6:35-36 (NIV)
15. Psalm 27:13
16. 1 Timothy 6:18-19
17. 2 Timothy 2:13
18. 1 Thessalonians 2:7-8
19. 1 Thessalonians 2:11-12 (NIV)
20. Matthew 11:28-30
21. Ephesians 1:18-21
22. 1 Corinthians 9:24,26-27
23. John 15:5
24. Psalms 34:1-3 (NIV)
25. 1 Samuel 21:10-15
26. Luke 6:45
27. Psalms 34:2-3 (NIV)
28. Psalm 34:4 (NIV)

Chapter 14—Keep on the Right Path to the Right One

1. Hebrews 13:5
2. Psalm 37:3-5
3. Habakkuk 3:17-19 (NIV)

Other Books
by Dick Purnell

■ ■ ■

A Personal Experiment in Faith-Building

Building a Biblical Self-Image

Building a Relationship That Lasts

Building a Strong Family

Free to Love Again:
Coming to Terms with Sexual Regret

Growing Closer to God

Knowing God by His Names

Knowing God's Heart, Sharing His Joy

Making a Good Marriage Even Better

Standing Strong in a Today's World

■ ■ ■

To order any of these books
visit: www.DickPurnell.com
or call (919) 363-8000

Other Good Harvest House Reading

■ ■ ■

Finding Your Perfect Mate
by H. Norman Wright
In this helpful book, Norm offers words of wisdom, encouragement, and guidance on one of life's most important decisions. Along with scriptural insights, he contributes valuable insights based on his years as a premarital counselor.

Sassy, Single, and Satisfied
by Michelle McKinney Hammond
With her humorous, tell-it-like-it-is style, Michelle combines scriptural principles for daily living with inspirational stories, quotes, and experiences of life, love, and men. Readers will find assurance that their singleness can be embraced and celebrated.

Secrets of an Irresistible Woman
by Michelle McKinney Hammond
Women will discover the rules and scriptural principles about love that ensure solid, godly relationships. Secrets offers practical advice, inspiring prayers, and study questions to help women understand and recognize real love.

Single Men are like Waffles, Single Women are like Spaghetti
by Bill and Pam Farrel
In this book, singles can explore the differences between men and women and learn to strengthen their relationships with members of the opposite sex.

What to Do Until Love Finds You
by Michelle McKinney Hammond
Drawing from her experience of being single and counseling single women, Michelle offers women practical, godly advice on how to handle sexual temptations regardless of past experience, develop internal and external beauty, and wait joyfully for God's timing.